"If you're highly sensitive, you've p[...]
Zeff's easy-to-follow advice will trans[...]
illuminating book on a critically important topic."

   —Linda Johnsen, MS, author of *The Complete*
     Idiot's Guide to Hinduism and *Alpha Teach*
     Yourself Yoga in Twenty-Four Hours

"This book is a must read for every highly sensitive person.
Zeff has many innovative techniques for coping with the
overstimulation and stress in our fast-paced world."

   —Sanford L. Severin, MD, author of *TriEnergetics*

The

HIGHLY SENSITIVE PERSON'S

Survival Guide

Essential Skills for Living Well in an Overstimulating World

TED ZEFF, PH.D.
Foreword by ELAINE N. ARON, PH.D.

New Harbinger Publications, Inc.

Publisher's Note

Are You Highly Sensitive? A Self-Test on page 4 is from THE HIGHLY SENSITIVE PERSON by Elaine Aron. Copyright © 1996 by Elaine N. Aron. A Citadel Press Book. All rights reserved. Reprinted by arrangement with Kensington Publishing Corp. www.kensingtonbooks.com

Distributed in Canada by Raincoast Books.

Copyright © 2004 by Ted Zeff
New Harbinger Publications, Inc.
5674 Shattuck Avenue
Oakland, CA 94609

Cover design by Amy Shoup
Edited by Carole Honeychurch
Acquired by Spencer Smith
Text design by Michele Waters-Kermes

ISBN 1-57224-396-1 Paperback

All Rights Reserved

Printed in the United States of America

New Harbinger Publications' Web site address: www.newharbinger.com

06   05   04

10   9   8   7   6   5   4   3   2   1

First printing

Contents

Foreword

$\mathcal{I}$ am happy to introduce this book to highly sensitive people (HSPs) and their loved ones. For those of you new to the concept, Ted Zeff does a fine job of making you acquainted with who HSPs are and how they operate in the world. In particular, his caring and respect comes through on every page.

Between these covers Ted Zeff shares many thoughtful insights, fine accounts of solutions to problems found by HSPs, and an excellent collection of fresh, practical suggestions for supporting the highly sensitive body and spirit. But most importantly, he models a caring, respectful attitude towards HSPs everywhere. We are fortunate to have his attention.

For those of you familiar with my work, you will find that Ted and I approach many things differently, but that may be very refreshing. It is important that we understand that although our nervous systems are similar in an essential way, we can approach problems and think about things very differently. The more sound perspectives that are available, the better, and Ted's perspective is a good one.

—Elaine N. Aron, Ph.D.

Preface

"*I* wish those neighbors would turn down their music. It's driving me crazy. I can't stand it anymore."

"What music? I don't hear a thing. You shouldn't let noise bother you. Something's wrong with you."

Actually nothing is wrong with you if you are sensitive to noise, scents, lights, or if you feel overwhelmed by crowds and time pressure or can't screen out stimuli. You may simply be part of the 15 to 20 percent of the population who are highly sensitive. Your high sensitivity may have presented challenges throughout your life. For instance, you may experience low self-esteem when you are told that you are flawed for being different or experience anxiety and tension when interacting with loud, aggressive people or are exposed to constant stimuli throughout the day. In this book, you will learn hundreds of coping techniques to survive and thrive in a non-HSP (highly sensitive person) world that values aggression and overstimulation. As you read this book and begin to implement the many new strategies it offers to manage your trait, you will come to appreciate your sensitivity and understand how beneficial it is to be an HSP.

This book is not only for highly sensitive people. Non-HSPs will benefit from reading this book by learning how to support their HSP friends and relatives. The coping strategies will also help non-HSPs experience more inner-peace in their life.

How I Came to Write This Book

I remember clearly that I began experiencing anxiety and insomnia when I was in fifth grade due to feeling overwhelmed in school. I couldn't screen out stimuli and became extremely anxious and tense in my large and noisy classroom. By the time I was in the seventh grade my school life had really deteriorated. I continuously experienced severe reactions in the classroom and experienced an almost total inability to concentrate on my schoolwork. My parents took me to a psychologist to find out why I was "overreacting," both at school and at home. Unfortunately, the non-HSP therapist didn't understand that I was highly sensitive and blamed me for my difficulty dealing with overstimulation.

Twenty years later, when I was studying for my Ph.D. in psychology, specializing in stress management, I discovered that my sensitivity and inability to screen out stimuli was the root cause of anxiety throughout my life. I began to realize that trying to fit into an aggressive, overstimulating world only exacerbated my tension. Therefore, I made important changes in my lifestyle. I began reducing my overstimulating behavior, maintained an exercise schedule that was appropriate for my constitution, changed my diet, and began implementing daily relaxation techniques. I also began to learn to appreciate and accept my sensitivity.

My postgraduate studies led me to investigate the fields of nutrition, meditation, and holistic healing for highly sensitive people. Based on my research and experimentation, I began teaching classes on stress management for medical groups, hospitals, and colleges. I now teach classes on coping strategies for highly sensitive people. It's a privilege to share with you the many coping techniques that have worked for both my highly sensitive students and myself.

What You Will Learn

In *The Highly Sensitive Person's Survival Guide* I will offer you the wisdom I have gained throughout my life as an HSP and as a psychologist. This includes an exploration into what "high sensitivity" means, especially in this fast-paced, overstimulating world. The book also includes practical techniques and strategies that will enable you to thrive as an HSP.

You will learn how the mores of our society reinforce a negative self-image for the HSP and how to appreciate your sensitivity. You will discover how to change habits that are detrimental to your inner-peace. I'll introduce specific meditative exercises to help you remain centered and peaceful throughout the day, and guide you in developing a detailed morning and evening routine that will help you cope with extraneous stimuli.

This book includes many methods to calm the senses, along with specific techniques to cope with time pressure. You will learn how to maintain a healthy body by creating an appropriate diet, exercise, and supplement plan that is specific for the highly sensitive person.

The relationship between overstimulation and sleep is an important one, and we'll be focusing on improving your sleep patterns. Then you'll learn innovative relaxation techniques to help you sleep better. How being a highly sensitive person influences your relationships may not have occurred to you, but it's an interesting and vital aspect of the highly sensitive life. Specific techniques to create harmonious relationships with your family, friends, and coworkers will be a welcome addition to your HSP toolbox.

We'll discuss the unique challenges for the HSP in today's competitive work environment and many solutions to cope with stress on the job. The program includes practical methods for changing a difficult work environment and suggestions for creating a new, stress-free job.

You'll begin to understand how your inherent capacity to have deep spiritual experiences can help you experience inner-peace. I'll offer practical information on how to nurture your sensitive soul and you'll begin to recognize the benefits of living from a spiritual perspective.

We'll examine many questions from HSPs on how to deal with difficult situations, and you'll learn practical solutions. Some of the questions include: coping with noisy, rude neighbors; getting along with difficult people at work, and dealing with relatives who disregard your sensitivity. The final chapter consists of a comprehensive guide of many healing options for the highly sensitive person. There is also a list of books and Web sites for HSPs.

Now that you know why I wrote this book and what you'll learn, it's time to begin your new journey toward inner-peace.

Acknowledgements

Elaine Aron 's pioneering work on highly sensitive people has made this book possible, and I appreciate all her support. I am grateful for all the students in my classes who shared their stories. I appreciate the editorial assistance of Jeanette Allen, Sharon Flowers, and Pam Jung. Kudos to Andy Shedd for his technical support and Linda Johnsen for her suggestions. I want to acknowledge my niece, Rebecca Anderman, who encouraged me to write this book, Carole Honeychurch, my excellent supportive copy editor, and Spencer Smith, my acquisitions editior, for his belief in this project. I am especially grateful to my spiritual teacher, Ammachi, whose unconditional love for all of humanity, has inspired me and millions of others to live a more compassionate, balanced, and joyful life.

1

An Introduction to Being an HSP

"I can't take the stress at work anymore. My coworker at the next desk talks all day long in a loud, abrasive voice, and my boss keeps demanding that I meet his rigid deadlines. I leave work every day feeling drained, and jittery, with my stomach tied up in knots."

"Everyone in my family is always running around trying some new adventure while I like to stay home. I feel like there's something wrong with me because I usually don't like to go out after work or on weekends."

Does any of this sound familiar to you? If so, you may be a highly sensitive person.

What Is a Highly Sensitive Person?

Since Elaine Aron's landmark book, *The Highly Sensitive Person,* was published in 1996, hundreds of thousands of HSPs (highly sensitive people) have begun to realize that they are not flawed for life due to their finely tuned nervous system. Approximately 15 to 20 percent of the population have trouble screening out stimuli and can be easily overwhelmed by noise, crowds, and time pressure. The HSP tends to be very sensitive to pain, the effects of caffeine, and violent movies. Highly sensitive people are also made extremely uncomfortable by bright lights, strong smells, and changes in their lives. In this companion book to *The Highly Sensitive Person,* you will learn hundreds of new coping strategies to remain calm and tranquil in today's overstimulating world, transforming your sensitivity into inner-peace and joy.

HSPs can find it challenging growing up in a society that values aggression and overstimulation. I grew up in the era of heroes such as John Wayne, when real men were supposed to be strong, tough, and silent. As a highly sensitive boy, I didn't fit in at school and felt that there was something inherently wrong with me. At an early age I surmised that I was a bad person because I believed the lie that being sensitive was disgusting. Virtually all of the emotional pain that I experienced growing up was directly related to a lack of understanding about my very sensitive nervous system.

As an adult, you may still suffer from a lack of understanding about your sensitivity. HSPs are adversely affected by our fast-paced and aggressive modern industrialized society. You can easily become exhausted, perpetually overstimulated by everything from the proliferation of violence in the media to the cacophony of loud urban noises. Since HSPs are a minority of the population, you may internalize the mores of our non-HSP society. Unfortunately, when you try to fit into an overstimulating, out-of-balance world, your physical, emotional, and spiritual health suffers.

The Highly Sensitive Person Questionnaire

When I took Elaine Aron's Highly Sensitive Person Self-Test many years ago I almost thought the questionnaire was designed specifically for me, as I immediately responded yes to every question. However, there are many differences amongst highly sensitive people. Some HSPs find noise intolerable but are not bothered by scents. Other HSPs can tune out noise, but are extremely bothered by bright lights.

The term "highly sensitive" may elicit either a positive or negative reaction. The thesaurus on my Microsoft Word program gives the following synonyms for sensitivity: compassion, sympathy, understanding, and kindliness. However, for some respondents I've interviewed, the words "highly sensitive" brought up feelings of shame and worthlessness, and I observed those interviewees trying to minimize their sensitivity during the HSP Self-Test.

Many progressive people now believe that sensitivity is a positive trait. Those respondents didn't want to appear "insensitive" when I administered the questionnaire, and I noticed that they would spend a long time answering each question, trying to justify their sensitivity. Try to be aware of your feelings about the term "highly sensitive" as you respond to the questions on the HSP Self-Test.

Are You Highly Sensitive? A Self-Test*

Answer each question according to the way you feel. Answer true if it is at least somewhat true for you. Answer false if it is not very true or not at all true for you.

I seem to be aware of subtleties in my environment.	T	F
Other people's moods affect me.	T	F
I tend to be very sensitive to pain.	T	F
I find myself needing to withdraw during busy days, into bed or into a darkened room or any place where I can have some privacy and relief from stimulation.	T	F
I am particularly sensitive to the effects of caffeine.	T	F
I am easily overwhelmed by things like bright lights, strong smells, coarse fabrics, or sirens close by.	T	F
I have a rich, complex inner life.	T	F
I am made uncomfortable by loud noises.	T	F
I am deeply moved by the arts or music.	T	F
I am conscientious.	T	F
I startle easily.	T	F
I get rattled when I have a lot to do in a short amount of time.	T	F
When people are uncomfortable in a physical environment I tend to know what needs to be done to make it more comfortable (like changing the lighting or the seating).	T	F
I am annoyed when people try to get me to do too many things at once.	T	F

---

*   From THE HIGHLY SENSITIVE PERSON by Elaine Aron. Copyright © 1996 by Elaine N. Aron. A Citadel Press Book. All rights reserved. Reprinted by arrangement with Kensington Publishing Corp. www.kensingtonbooks.com

I try hard to avoid making mistakes or forgetting things.   T   F

I make it a point to avoid violent movies and TV shows.   T   F

I become unpleasantly aroused when a lot is going on   T   F
around me.

Being very hungry creates a strong reaction in me,   T   F
disrupting my concentration or mood.

Changes in my life shake me up.   T   F

I notice and enjoy delicate or fine scents, tastes, sounds,   T   F
works of art.

I make it a high priority to arrange my life to avoid   T   F
upsetting or overwhelming situations.

When I must compete or be observed while performing a   T   F
task, I become so nervous or shaky that I do much worse
than I would otherwise.

When I was a child, my parents or teachers seemed to see   T   F
me as sensitive or shy.

Scoring Yourself

If you answered true to twelve or more of the questions, you're probably highly sensitive. But frankly, no psychological test is so accurate that you should base your life on it. If only one or two questions are true of you but they are extremely true, you might also be justified in calling yourself highly sensitive.

The HSP's Nervous System

In an interview on November 10, 2003 with Carolyn Robertson, certified neurotherapist, I discovered that the HSP's brain wave patterns are more frequently in a theta state. In this state, a person is more open to intuitive feelings and to picking up light, sound, and other subtle vibrations more deeply. While deep meditators (regardless of their sensitivity) are frequently in a theta state, they are able to filter out sensations through concentration.

However, when not focused inward, HSPs are processing stimulation so thoroughly that they are easily overwhelmed, far sooner than non-HSPs. One could say that they have trouble tuning out irrelevant stimuli—except who is to say what is irrelevant? Noticing where an exit sign is located can seem irrelevant until there is a fire.

HSPs have to learn to ignore or protect themselves from unwanted stimuli. Especially those of us who have had a difficult childhood report a chronic, painful inability to avoid overstimulation (Aron 1996). Donna, an attractive and intelligent woman in her mid-forties, was a student in one of my HSP classes. She told me that she sometimes feels as if she is walking around with no skin, like a sponge absorbing everything that comes her way. She commented that as a child she also felt like she had no protection from the barrage of negative stimulation at home and at school, resulting in her experiencing severe emotional reactions to the daily assault on her nervous system.

Donna courageously shared with the class how her parents took her to a neurologist when she was thirteen. Donna's EEG (electroencephalogram) indicated an erratic brain wave pattern that may have contributed to her intense reaction to stimuli. The neurologist recommended that she take medication to reduce her intense reaction to stimuli, and Donna felt that the medicine probably helped. However, in retrospect, she noted that if she had grown up in a supportive and loving environment where her sensitivity was understood and accepted, she wouldn't have had such intense emotional reactions and wouldn't have needed medication. While medication can be helpful in some situations, I recommend that you first implement a holistic approach in coping with your sensitive nervous system.

Societal Values and Sensitivity

In the last ten to twenty years there has been more acceptance of sensitivity and some wonderful improvements in societal values. Although most men have been brought up to act tough and repress emotions, many progressive men now feel that sensitivity is a positive characteristic. In recent years the media has been featuring many stories about the relationship between stress-related diseases and intense work environments, giving people the opportunity to question whether working under severe pressure is worth harming their health.

While there is now a subculture of progressive people who accept sensitivity as a cherished value for both men and women, over-stimulation in our society has increased at an alarming rate. A popular song in the 60s was the innocent *I Want to Hold Your Hand*, while today the accepted raucous music is frequently filled with lyrics of swearing and violence. One of the worst offenses in school a generation ago was cutting classes, while now there are security guards and metal detectors at many urban schools to prevent school shootings.

In the 1950s there were three or four television stations, while today we are inundated with up to one thousand stations broadcasting a multitude of shows saturated with graphic sex and gratuitous violence. The home telephone has been replaced by millions of cell phones, ubiquitous to modern society, and creating a cacophony of clamor throughout the world. Recently I was hiking on top of a magnificent mountain peak in Colorado, enjoying the peaceful and spectacular natural setting when a man charged by me screaming into his cell phone, "I told you to sell the stock."

Thirty or forty years ago most people shopped at small neighborhood stores and had a personal relationship with the storeowner or clerk. In most urban environments, virtually all mom-and-pop stores have been replaced by gigantic, impersonal corporations, which could be called "Stimulation Depot" or "Noise R Us." You have to fight with hordes of other shoppers as you desperately search for bargains amongst thousands of items or wander around trying to find assistance from the few overwhelmed and underpaid clerks. Given this intense level of stimulation, you can understand why HSPs often find shopping nowadays an emotionally exhausting experience. I remember seeing one cartoon that depicted a young woman shopping for toothpaste. She became overwhelmed when trying to choose from a multitude of toothpaste brands: anticavity, fluoride, no fluoride, antigingivitis, extra whitener, gel, striped, antistain for smokers, protection for gums, 15 percent savings on large, 20 percent savings on extra large. After reviewing the multitude of products to choose from, she felt so overwhelmed that she went home to lie down from exhaustion.

Age is a factor in determining our sensitivity to stimuli. Children and older people are more deeply affected by overstimulation. Since children haven't yet developed the capacity to express themselves, they frequently react intensely. (For more information about highly sensitive children read *The Highly Sensitive Child* by Dr. Elaine Aron, in which she succinctly describes the unique challenges of raising sensitive children). As teenagers and young adults, HSPs have a higher tolerance for overstimulation. Some HSP teenagers usually can even tolerate listening to loud music and partying to all hours of the night. As you age, your capacity for stimulation decreases, and it's common for many middle-aged HSPs to go to bed early and avoid going out much. However, you always need to find a balance between too much and too little stimulation. After the age of sixty-five, your ability to tolerate stimuli is further diminished.

Since most countries value aggressive behavior, adjusting to non-HSP values is challenging for the sensitive person in most societies. The HSP's adjustment is dependent on the culture in which they were raised. In a study of Canadian and Chinese school children, it was found that in Canada highly sensitive children were the least liked and respected, while in China sensitive children were the most popular (Aron 2002). I had a foreign exchange student from Thailand who lived with me for a year. Tone was a sixteen-year old sensitive, gentle boy when he came to the United States. He told me that the Thai people value kindness and gentleness. Most Thai people speak and walk softly and are perhaps the gentlest people in the world. When I observed him talking with his Thai friends, I noticed that they would speak in soft, melodic voices. It was very difficult for Tone to adjust to an aggressive American high school environment, where tough and bellicose behavior in males was valued while gentleness and sensitivity was considered a flaw. Tone learned to deny his sensitivity and tried to become more assertive in order to survive in the non-HSP Western culture.

Countries vary regarding how much stimulation their citizens are exposed to. One study indicated that the Dutch keep their infants calmer than Americans, who generally expose their babies to more stimulation (Aron 2002). In India, children are brought up with a great deal of stimulation, making it challenging for the HSP. However, even sensitive people in India become more habituated to hearing incessant noise. I interviewed a highly sensitive man from India who had lived in the United States for five years. Ramesh reported that the longer that he stayed in America, the more acculturated he became to the comparatively quiet atmosphere, and it was difficult for him when he visited India. However, since he was raised in an extremely noisy environment, he told me that he eventually adapts to the overstimulation of his native country, and after some time the excessive noise doesn't bother him so much.

While HSPs who are raised in overstimulating environments can cope more easily with excessive stimuli, sensitive people brought up in less stimulating societies have a more difficult time adapting. A highly sensitive American woman told me about a spiritual tour of India that she attended with both Westerners and Indians, and her story illustrated how Americans need their quiet space. She said that the Indian and American women slept on the floor in two different large rooms. In one room all the Indian women slept together in one corner touching each other, like a litter of puppies, while all the American women slept exactly three feet apart from each other in the other room.

Likewise, if an HSP from rural Montana moved to Manhattan, she would become easily overwhelmed by the assault on her senses. In the opposite case, sensitive people who have become habituated to urban overstimulation may have difficulty adjusting to a quiet, rural environment. When I lived in the bucolic Sierra Mountains in California, I had a friend who worked in downtown San Francisco visit me for the weekend. The lack of stimulation made him anxious, and he wanted to go to the nearest town, thirty minutes away. One HSP student who lives in a noisy urban neighborhood told me that she had trouble sleeping due to the quiet on a recent visit to the country.

Thank Goodness for Sensitive People

By understanding, accepting, and appreciating your sensitive nervous system and by learning practical methods to deal with your sensitivity, you will gradually be able to identify and release any internalized false beliefs that there is something inherently wrong with you. HSPs are a large minority in this society that values and thrives on overstimulation, competition, and aggression. However, in order for a society to function at an optimal level there has to be a balance between the non-HSP soldiers and chief executive officers and the mostly HSP counselors and artists.

As a matter of fact, if there were more HSPs, we would probably live in a healthier world, with less war, environmental devastation, and terrorism. It is the HSP whose sensitivity helps create restrictions on smoking, pollution, and noise. However, it's important to note that there are very compassionate and kind non-HSPs and rude and insensitive HSPs. As a matter of fact, my non-HSP dad was one of the most considerate and caring people that I've even known.

While most non-HSPs are kindhearted, the aggressive traits of non-HSPs are exalted in the media in most societies. Some of the non-HSP chief executive officers of the major corporations have severely damaged the planet with indiscriminate oil drilling, clear cutting of forests, and pollution of the environment. The highly sensitive person has an important mission, which is to serve as a balance to the more aggressive behavior of some of the non-HSPs who advocate a less than nurturing policy toward humans, animals, and Mother Nature. Although you may have been told that you are too sensitive, the truth is that the proliferation of insensitive values has created a world on the brink of disaster, and our only hope for saving the planet is by being sensitive and kind toward all sentient beings.

Although our trait can be challenging, some of the marvelous benefits of being an HSP may include the following: We are conscientious and have the capacity to deeply appreciate beauty, art, and music. We can also really appreciate delicious food, due to our sensitive taste buds, our sensitive sense of smell helps us deeply enjoy aromatic, natural scents, such as flowers. We are intuitive and tend to have deep spiritual experiences. We will notice potential danger, such as immediately feeling a tick crawling on our skin, sooner than non-HSPs. We are very aware of safety issues and will be the first one to know how to exit a building in case of an emergency. We are concerned about the humane treatment of animals. We tend to be kind, compassionate, and understanding, making us natural counselors, teachers, and healers. We have an enthusiasm for life and thus can experience love and joy more deeply than non-HSPs, if we aren't feeling overwhelmed.

The majority, non-HSP culture sometimes negatively judges our sensitivity. The HSP is a minority in all societies, which usually favor the majority non-HSPs (Aron 1996). You may be occasionally told by non-HSPs that there is something wrong with you when you express the need for quiet time or when you're feeling overwhelmed at work or taking care of your duties at home. Being judged for having a finely tuned nervous system is like discriminating against people based on the color of their skin, religion, or national origin. Like other minority groups, it's important that we strive to educate the general population about our sensitive nervous system, accept our sensitivity, and learn ways to cope in the majority non-HSP culture.

While you don't have to demonstrate, carrying placards that read "Sensitivity Power!" (you probably couldn't tolerate the noise and stimulation of a demonstration anyway), it would be beneficial to learn ways to raise your self-esteem. By reading books on HSPs (Elaine Aron's *The Highly Sensitive Person's Workbook* is a magnificent way to reframe your childhood in light of your sensitivity), attending individual therapy or HSP groups or classes to understand your trait, and employing many of the suggestions in this book, you will improve your self-esteem. Develop new friendships with other HSPs and try not to spend time with judgmental non-HSPs who make you feel flawed. It's also very important not to compare yourself or try to compete with non-HSPs.

Coping As an HSP

If you're told that you are too sensitive, it's good to have a prepared rebuttal available. You could tell the non-HSP, "According to research by Dr. Elaine Aron, HSPs are thought to be found in approximately 20 percent of the population (equally divided between male and female). This population has a more finely tuned central nervous system, so we are more susceptible to environmental stimuli, both positive and negative. The stimuli could be noise, fragrance, bright lights, beauty, time pressure, or pain. We tend to process sensory stimuli more deeply than most people. It can be an enjoyable and challenging trait to have." One note of caution is that it's important to use your discrimination when telling others about your sensitivity. If you think the other person would ridicule or discount your sensitivity, it's best not to share the information. I've had some HSP students tell me that their family or coworkers disregarded their explanations about their sensitivity, making them feel worse.

Since you are living in a majority non-HSP culture, it's important to learn the art of compromise and not expect people to always make major lifestyle changes to accommodate you. One HSP reported that she had some neighbors in her urban apartment building playing their music loudly every evening. She told me that she negotiated a compromise with them so that the music would be low during the week, but on Friday and Saturday nights they could play the music louder during certain hours.

It's important for you to be polite when asking people to make changes when you feel overwhelmed and not to blame anyone who enjoys excessive stimuli. It's also beneficial to have a prepared statement when asking for what you need from others. For example, if you're asking someone to be quieter, try to develop a positive relationship with the person before asking or writing them with your request to make less noise. After explaining to the other person that you have a noise sensitivity, tell the person that you want to make sure that they are comfortable and not inconvenienced by your request. Tell the individual how much you would appreciate it if they could be quiet at certain times. Then ask the person to let you know if there is anything you could do to help make their life easier. Finally, you may want to apologize for any inconvenience the request may have on the person's life and thank them for being so kind and considerate.

It's essential for you to accept your sensitivity and not emulate non-HSP behavior. I remember flying from California to St. Louis for a family reunion and feeling exhausted from the stimulating trip. When we arrived at my sister's home, my non-HSP son, David, joined the other non-HSP relatives in going out for a late night movie, while I needed to immediately withdraw into a quiet, dark room to rest. By not going out with my non-HSP relatives, I was able to recuperate from the stimulating journey.

HSPs feel pain more deeply then non-HSPs and many have reported that when they experience physical pain, they immediately investigate what is causing the problem and attempt to alleviate the discomfort. Non-HSPs can generally tolerate more pain. A non-HSP friend told me that he had broken his foot, but was able to ignore the pain for over a month, even as he worked as a carpenter. Stoicism doesn't work for HSPs.

You need to find a balance between creating too much stimulation, which causes anxiety, and too little stimulation, which results in boredom. For example, if you find the stimulation of crowds in movie theaters too overwhelming, you can choose to see a movie during non-peak hours (such as matinees on weekdays). You can always rent a video, although some HSPs have reported that trying to select a nonviolent video in the often-hectic environment of most video stores quite challenging. You can also go to restaurants before the dinner rush. Many restaurants have an early bird special that will allow you to have both a calmer and a cheaper dining experience.

You need to use discrimination about when to push yourself to deal with stimulation and when to avoid being overwhelmed. Sometimes you need to push yourself to go on a hike or visit a museum (during non-peak hours) rather than constantly escaping to the quiet and sanctity of your home. George, an HSP in his forties, went to an amusement park with his son, Julian. George told me that Julian begged him to join him in a go-cart race. He told his son that he couldn't deal with the stimulation of circumambulating a track in a dangerous racecar. However, since Julian was quite persistent, George finally agreed to try driving the racecar. He cautiously got the feel of the car and track, pausing to check out all the potential dangers. As George began to feel more secure, he actually started driving faster and felt exhilarated after the race.

When I lived in a rural environment I had the opportunity to learn how to drive a tractor. Although I was initially hesitant to try operating such a dangerous piece of equipment, I felt a sense of satisfaction after mastering this skill. However, I don't think there is an HSP heavy equipment operator union that I could join.

It's okay to say no to participating in stimulating activities if you would rather pursue a relaxing hobby such as drawing, writing, or reading. Some people in our culture pursue a constant craving for intense outer-stimulation to avoid going inward to explore their inner-self. It's beneficial for HSPs to spend some time every day meditating or pursuing quiet activities to balance life in our overstimulating world.

Sometimes you may be more overwhelmed by stimulation when you feel powerless. I have noticed that when HSPs are in control of how much stimulation that they are exposed to, it doesn't bother them as much. Robert is a middle-aged HSP who simply can't tolerate any noise in his environment. He lives in a remote country setting and rarely leaves his home. Robert has created an ideal situation to reduce stimulation by working out of his home office in a serene rural environment. I recently visited Robert and his wife while construction workers were remodeling their home. I found the noise from the constant hammering and use of power tools extremely disconcerting and was surprised that Robert wasn't bothered by the excessive noise. He told me that it didn't bother him because he knew that whenever he wanted the carpenters to be quiet, he could tell them to stop working.

Similarly, it drives me crazy to hear a barking dog, yet when my dog would bark, it never bothered me since I knew that I could stop the noise at any time. Perhaps when you are in an overstimulating situation a good question to ask yourself would be how you can feel more in control of circumstances rather than being a victim of the stimuli. Anger is based on feeling powerless and as soon as you empower yourself, the anger generally dissipates.

Sensitive Men

Sensitive men have particular challenges in aggressive Western cultures. Males are taught from an early age to act tough and not to express their emotions. According to William Pollock, the author of *Real Boys*, whenever boys do not conform to the "boy code" and instead show their gentleness and emotions, they are usually ostracized and humiliated (1998). Highly sensitive boys learn to deny their real selves in order to be accepted and approved by their peers. This denial can create fear, anxiety, and low self-esteem. Paul Kivel has written in his book *Men's Work* that boys are put into a "act like a man box," which means that they must be aggressive, tough, strong, in control, and active. According to Dan Kindlon and Michael Thompson, authors of *Raising Cain* (about protecting the emotional life of boys), if boys express emotions such as fear, anxiety, or sadness, they are seen as feminine, and the adults around them typically treat them in ways that suggest that such emotions are not normal for a boy (1999).

One highly sensitive man, Dan, told me that when he used to go to the movies with his friends as a boy, he would pretend to really enjoy the bloody and violent scenes while secretly looking away from the screen. He was always afraid that some of the other boys would see him avoiding the screen and tease him. He also shared with me that he was humiliated for not following the current sporting events when he was in junior high school. One time another boy sitting next to Dan asked him how he liked the big game and when Dan responded that he didn't know there was a game, the other boy started laughing at him and told the other boys that Dan was a nerd. Dan then decided to spend every day reading the sports page in order to feel accepted by the other boys. Dan also told me that he didn't like fighting. However, he attended martial arts lessons in order to not be physically abused by aggressive boys in high school. While most sensitive boys would not be attracted to violent sports like boxing, learning martial arts may be beneficial for some sensitive boys to learn so they won't be hurt or humiliated by violent bullies.

In our society, being sensitive is generally associated with being feminine and weak and can be quite emasculating for males. Sometimes sensitive men have internalized the false belief that there is something wrong with them because they are gentle and can't tolerate stimulation. One sensitive man told me that he was taught as a boy that he shouldn't let anything bother him. He did his best to follow a stereotypical "masculine" like style by working out every day at the gym, having a good sex life with his wife, and denying his sensitivity. However, he constantly experienced anxiety from emulating non-HSP male values.

Alex is an HSP father of a twelve-year old HSP son, Noah. Even though Alex suffered as a boy for not conforming to the boy code of acting tough, he felt animosity toward Noah whenever his son appeared weak. Noah's soft and gentle demeanor reminded Alex of how he suffered as a boy when he was teased and humiliated for his sensitivity. Even though he knew it was wrong, Alex pushed Noah to go out for the football team and pursue traditional masculine activities even though Noah had no interest in sports. Noah became traumatized when trying to compete with the other football players and quit going to practices. At his mother's urging, the family entered counseling. Once Alex began attending family counseling sessions, he realized that he was forcing his son to deny his gentleness due to an internalized self-loathing for his own sensitivity. After some time, Alex was able to accept Noah—and himself—as highly sensitive males.

Changing Habits

How and why to change your habits is perhaps one of the most important things you'll learn in this book. You can read about all sorts of helpful healing modalities, but if you don't integrate the new methods into your daily routine, the healing techniques will fade from your memory. Reading a guidebook without applying the new concepts is like taking a boat across a river, but not getting out on the other side. In this section you will learn how to implement the many healing methods you'll be learning in this book.

The first step in changing habits is to investigate how your belief system influences your behavior. When you were a child, you were probably taught by your parents, teachers, peers, and the media that you can only be happy if you live a stimulating life based on outer gratification, such as making a lot of money, finding the perfect mate, and achieving success at work. Looking for happiness and trying to obtain a feeling of self-worth exclusively from outside stimuli can create anxiety and tension for the reflective, sensitive person.

It's vital to deeply examine your life goals as you begin to understand that what you truly desire is inner-peace and that nothing in this constantly changing world can really give you lasting contentment. Life is temporary, and everything will eventually leave you. You can't take money, a partner, or job status with you when you leave your body, so begin to look inside to make the necessary changes that will create inner-peace and happiness today.

As a child, you were probably told that there was something inherently wrong with you for being so sensitive. You may have internalized that false belief, creating an addictive, self-fulfilling prophecy, subconsciously identifying with emotional pain. In other words, whenever you are confronted with sensitivity challenges, you may subconsciously believe that you deserve to suffer since you think that you're flawed. Most self-defeating behavior is based on not loving yourself (Hay 1987). I frequently encounter sensitive students who have told me that it's difficult to let go of an untenable situation, even when it's creating enormous pain in their lives. There was a highly sensitive woman whose noisy upstairs neighbors were driving her crazy, yet she would always come up with an excuse not to move. I knew another HSP who worked for an abusive boss yet steadfastly refused to look for another job. Most people who remain in emotionally destructive situations believe that they deserve to suffer. Their low self-esteem, which is based on the untruth that there is something wrong with them, makes them think that pain is their due.

Once you begin to understand the basis of your belief system, you will be aware of how your internalized beliefs influence your thought patterns. In other words, when you sow a thought, you reap an action. When you repeat an action, you develop a habit. When you maintain a habit, you create a character.

When changing habits you need to be gentle with yourself and make the changes slowly. For example, if you try to stop an overeating habit cold turkey by going on a crash diet, you may end up eating the cold turkey—and all the trimmings. Take changes step by step. For example, if you want to go to bed an hour earlier to obtain more sleep, try going to bed just five minutes earlier each night so that in a few weeks, you'll reach your goal.

Once you have changed your consciousness by internalizing new positive values, you will spontaneously make changes to create more inner-peace and joy in your life. I was a TV addict my entire life until 1992. Even though I tried creating a healthier lifestyle for myself through exercise, a healthy diet, regular meditation, and employing new spiritual values, I would still watch shows that were detrimental to my emotional health for hours every day. The remote control was like a drug in my hands, as my thumb would compulsively flip from station to station. One night I was watching a movie based on a true story about a mass murderer who killed employees in an office building. Suddenly, I asked myself if I would invite this evil person into my living room if he knocked on my door. No way! Then I asked myself why I was allowing him into my home through the television. When the movie ended I took down my antenna and never watched commercial TV at home again. In retrospect, what finally broke my detrimental television addiction was a change in my consciousness: a realization of how destructive watching

TV was for me as a highly sensitive person and that it would not bring me the inner-peace I desired.

If you watch a few videos or limit your television time to several spiritually uplifting shows a week, it would mean spending considerably less time being overstimulated than the typical American (who watches approximately four hours of television daily). Another advantage to decreasing your time in front of the television is avoiding being bombarded by a myriad of endless overarousing commercials. The advertisers are trying to sell us their product in the least amount of time possible, resulting in a assault of stimuli that can wreak havoc with an HSP's finely tuned nervous system. When watching television, remember to mute the commercials.

It's much easier to change habits when you are receiving support from other people than trying to make the changes alone. For example, I asked my family to help me maintain an environment free of commercial TV in my home. Besides enlisting support from your relatives, friends, and coworkers, you can attend a support group such as a twelve-step program or individual counseling. Once you have instituted new, positive habits in your life, you will become a shining example for both HSPs and non-HSPs , motivating others to seek inner-peace.

You'll need to use your will power to change habits. Make a list of the areas that are causing you pain, and as you read this book, use your volition to write down the new methods that you will employ to address these areas. As you begin having small victories in changing habits, your willpower will be strengthened. You can also increase your inner-strength through visualization and the use of affirmations. Make a resolution today that you will no longer remain in any environment in which there is no hope for you to be happy.

However, since environment may be stronger than your willpower to change, you also need to remove yourself from situations that reinforce negative habits and low self-esteem. Your home and work environment are the most important factors that determine your ability to create a peaceful life, so it's imperative that you create a harmonious work and home atmosphere. If you know that a certain environment creates anxiety, either try to change the unhealthy, overstimulating situation or remove yourself from the source of tension.

I have noticed that you can generally replace a bad habit with a good one in just six months. One HSP, Felicia, told me that after several months of meditating the practice became a part of her life, just like brushing her teeth when she awoke. Felicia said that if she is unable to meditate in the morning, she doesn't feel centered until she experiences at least ten minutes of deep relaxation. She noticed that when she's feeling calm, little daily annoyances become less significant. Once you become focused on establishing peace of mind, you won't have to give others a piece of your mind.

Finally, you need to create new, satisfying, and nurturing activities to replace old habits. For example, when I finally turned off the TV, I started to really enjoy reading inspiring books, writing stories, and listening to uplifting music. When I think of the thousands of hours that I wasted staring at inane, stimulating programs, I sometimes become saddened at how I increased tension and angst in my life. However, I also realize that I was doing the best I could given the knowledge that I had at that particular time. This is also a time of new beginnings for you, and you don't have to keep repeating old habits that don't work for you anymore as you gain new knowledge and understanding of yourself (Hay 1987).

How to Change Habits

- Investigate your belief system, and become aware when a habit creates pain.

- Be gentle with yourself by changing habits slowly.

- Try to always be aware of your new goal: creating inner-peace in your life.

- Enlist the support of your family, friends, co-workers, and neighbors; you may want to meet with a counselor or join a support group.

- Remove yourself from an environment that reinforces negative habits.

- Realize that in only six months you can replace a bad habit with a good one through daily practice.

- ⚕ Create new, satisfying, and nurturing activities to re-place old habits.

- ⚕ Using your willpower, develop a structured program to help you make positive lifestyle changes.

How to Use this Book

The goal of this book is to help the highly sensitive person learn coping strategies to remain calm and peaceful in today's overstimulating world. You will be given many suggestions on how to live a harmonious life and thrive at an optimal level. However, don't pressure yourself to feel that you have to integrate the hundreds of recommendations into your life. Even if you choose to employ only one or two of the suggestions, it will help you to become a happier person.

As you are reading this book it will be helpful for you to jot down notes regarding which methods you want to integrate into your life. You may want to use a journal so you don't forget any important suggestions. At the end of each chapter make a list of the techniques that you want to implement and put them on your calendar. Begin enjoying the new coping strategies by practicing them this week.

The key to a happy life for the HSP is planning ahead. It's very important to make the necessary preparations to reduce stimulation in advance, such as taking earplugs or a headset with you when you are going into a noisy environment. You need to remain vigilant so that you're not swept up in a sea of stifling societal stimulation. And finally, though it may sound strange, you may actually crave negative stimula-tion when you are out of balance. As you read the book, look deeply inside yourself to determine if your behavior is creating harmony or ten-sion in your life.

Welcome to the inner journey of exploring your psyche and emo-tions as you learn new and exciting methods to bring more inner-peace and joy into your life.

---------- *2* ----------

Preparing for Overstimulation in Your Daily Life

I was recently sitting in my car at a traffic light and noticed a very nervous-looking young woman in the car next to mine. Her radio was blasting loud rap music as she shrieked into her cell phone while simultaneously smoking a cigarette. She then flicked her cigarette butt out the window and took a gulp from a huge cup of coffee. As the light changed she quickly put down the cup and floored the gas pedal while still shouting into her cell phone. The car in front of hers was evidently moving a little too slowly for her temperament, so she began frantically honking her horn.

As an HSP, just watching the stimulation at the traffic light made me so anxious that I could feel the muscles in my body becoming tense as my hand grasped the steering wheel tighter. As mentioned in chapter 1, we are living in a fast-paced, stimuli-saturated world that is particularly challenging for highly sensitive people. As you can see from the story, highly sensitive people have difficulty being around stimulation. In this chapter you will learn many techniques to remain calm in overstimulating situations.

When I teach classes on stress-reduction, I ask the students what they think is the most common way people cope with stress. Some of the responses offered are the following: drinking alcohol, taking medication, shopping, watching television, working, surfing the Internet, and sleeping. Rarely does anyone come up with the correct answer, which is denial. For a non-HSP, it's dangerous to deny the detrimental effects of stress and overstimulation, but for an HSP it can be catastrophic.

I remember waiting in line at a store to pick up some business cards. The clerk was working alone behind the counter while the phone was ringing off the hook as more customers joined the queue. An irate customer demanded that his cards should have been ready that day. The frazzled clerk's face turned red as his voice began trembling with frustration and anger. When I stepped up to the desk, I tried to make him feel calmer by telling him that it must be difficult working all alone in such a stressful environment. In an irritated voice, he curtly responded that the pressure didn't bother him. However, time urgent behavior can create emotional and physical problems in our frenetic, fast-paced society.

Our Type A Society

Drs. Friedman and Rosenman wrote in their well-known book, *Type A Behavior and Your Heart* that the values of our society encourage Type A behavior (1974). According to Friedman and Rosenman, "Type A behavior has three main components: time urgency, excessive competitiveness, and hostility." Conversely, the Type B personality is characterized by the following traits: a relatively small sense of time urgency, noncompetitiveness, and lack of aggression.

Type A behavior is ubiquitous in America and industrialized countries today. In many studies over the last thirty years, it was found that the majority of participants were diagnosed as Type A while only a small minority exhibited Type B characteristics (Zeff 1981). According to Ethel Roskies, noted researcher of Type A intervention studies, the Type A characteristics of ambition, being goal-oriented, and time urgency are qualities that American society encourages.

While a highly sensitive person could be either Type A or Type B, the HSP is deeply affected by our Type A culture. The HSP can become easily overwhelmed and usually performs poorly when pressured by time, competition, and aggressive behavior. Since the HSP is easily affected by other people's moods, you may have a tendency to internalize the mores of our Type A culture.

Even the non-HSP can be negatively affected by time urgency pressure that is endemic in today's work place. According to Dr. Rosenman, if a Type A person succeeds in a task, it is in spite of the Type A behavior, not because of it. Interestingly, D.C. Glass reported in the *Journal of Applied Social Psychology* (1974) that the Type A subjects were less successful than the Type Bs in performing job-related tasks.

The Need to Disengage

As an HSP, you'll need to utilize specific behavior modification exercises to disengage from the Type A environment. Techniques such as meditation and deep breathing will help you disconnect from the fast-paced world we're living in. Unfortunately, most people don't want to modify their lifestyle, even if it's causing them tension and anxiety. However, one of the few groups of Type A people who have always been willing to attempt change were those who experienced a heart attack. When the doctors told those patients that if they didn't make immediate changes in their lifestyle they would die, the post-coronary heart patients participated in a Type A modification program. Ah, now there's motivation to change! Likewise, HSPs should act as if their life depends on modifying Type A beliefs. If you don't implement lifestyle changes, you may be damaging both your physical and emotional health.

Reacting to Challenges

It's important for the HSP to realize that even if you cannot control the Type A environment, you do have the power to control your reaction to it. In this chapter you will learn various techniques, such as meditation and following a daily routine, that will help you cope with seemingly untenable situations. You can always take meditation breaks throughout the day and do slow abdominal breathing. Research consistently has shown that people who meditate experience significantly less stress than nonmeditators. In my research of Type A personalities, I observed that meditators had a decreased heart rate, systolic blood pressure, and anxiety level at a statistically significant level compared to a control group of nonmeditators (Zeff 1981).

Besides regular meditation, practicing specific techniques must be implemented to release the time urgency aspect of Type A behavior. In addition to the techniques offered in this book, you may want to try individual or group counseling, attending a Type A reduction class (usually given to post-coronary patients at hospitals), or attending a stress-reduction class. One of the benefits of the HSP's characteristic of being conscientious is the ability to follow through with integrating new techniques into your life to reduce stimulation. By regularly practicing stress-reduction exercises, you will lead a healthier and happier life.

Attitude is Everything

Before you begin learning the techniques that will help you cope more effectively in this Type A world, let's look at how your attitude affects your sense of well being. The HSP's desire to be conscientious and not make mistakes can create stress. When I was studying how to differentiate various personality types with Dr. Ray Rosenman, I remember listening to a recording of a Type A man. He had a relatively simple job with the post office. When asked if there was a lot of pressure in his job, he responded tensely "definitely." He had to put letters into different boxes depending on the zip code. He frequently became upset if he thought that he placed a letter in the wrong box. Throughout the tape as he discussed his job duties, he became more agitated.

Next, I listened to a recording of a man who was the CEO of a multimillion dollar corporation. He calmly stated that his job wasn't stressful because he would simply write down his agenda each morning and complete the activities he had time for and delegate the other duties to his subordinates. If he didn't finish a project, he wouldn't worry about it. While certain jobs can create tension, the attitude that we bring to a job is the major factor that determines our level of stress.

These examples illustrate the importance of developing a positive attitude of acceptance rather than worrying if you have completed a job adequately. One HSP student told me that she would become extremely upset if she felt that she made a mistake at work. She would agonize for hours about the possible errors she committed. After working with her for several months, she began to slowly change her attitude realizing that she could only do her best and try to let go of her need to complete each task perfectly. In the chapters ahead you will learn techniques to help you come to this level of peace.

I hope reading about our overstimulating world doesn't overwhelm you! Just take a deep, slow breath right now, and realize that you are learning new coping skills so that you can more easily deal with our Type A society.

Creating a Morning Routine

While you can't live your life totally removed from the world's jolts, you can create an environment that minimizes stimuli. If you can anchor yourself to a ship of tranquility, you won't be tossed about by the waves of stimulation.

One of the most important steps in reducing stimulation for the HSP is to create a morning routine. This structure will set the tone for your entire day and your evening routine will influence the quality of your sleep. If you arise late in the morning, hurriedly grab a cup of coffee for breakfast, and rush to your job, you're setting yourself up for tension throughout the day. However, by waking up only twenty minutes earlier and performing centering activities, you can begin your day in a serene and peaceful state. Then you will be better prepared to handle stimuli throughout the day

Exercising Your Body

It's good to do some gentle stretching, yoga postures, or light calisthenics when you first awaken. Performing some physical activity upon arising has an energizing effect on the body. You may want to start your morning routine with some yoga postures. Yoga brings you into a natural state of tranquility and can improve the endocrine metabolism, which reduces stress and stress-related disorders (Lad 1984). Initially, you may want to take a class in hatha yoga to learn the proper techniques. Hatha yoga is not merely a physical exercise, the purpose of hatha yoga is to calm the body and mind in preparation for meditation. When studying yoga, be very gentle with yourself and never push yourself into a posture; only go into a posture as far as is comfortable for you.

Calming Your Mind

Once your body has been energized, try to do at least fifteen minutes of some type of meditative practice. You may want to do slow abdominal breathing. The following is a very simple five-minute practice that you can do in the morning or any time throughout the day.

Deep Breathing Exercise

Sit in a comfortable position and close your eyes. Inhale slowly through your nose into your abdomen to the count of five . . . hold to the count of five . . . and slowly exhale to the count of five . . . Feel your body becoming more and more relaxed with each exhalation . . .

Repeat the slow, deep breathing exercise again . . . really experience how calm and peaceful your body feels with each exhalation . . . Just observe the thoughts when they arise . . . then calmly return to your breathing . . . Inhale peace and calmness . . . hold . . . exhale any stress . . .

During the breathing exercise you can mentally repeat a mantra, such as the word "peace" or "calm" with each inhalation and each exhalation. You may find it more comfortable to inhale to a count of less than five seconds. Arrange the timing of your breath so that it feels comfortable to you.

Once you're feeling calm, you may want to begin progressive relaxation, which is performed by visualizing all of the muscles in your body relaxing deeper and deeper. You can begin by relaxing your scalp, facial muscles, and jaw. Then continue relaxing all parts of your body down to your feet. With each exhalation, visualize the muscles becoming softer and softer. If you have difficulty concentrating on these techniques, listening to a relaxation tape or CD is an excellent way to begin your day. You may want to listen to either my relaxation CD (www.hspsurvival.com), another personal favorite, or one you record for yourself using these techniques.

Since HSPs are so easily affected by other people's moods, it's important to practice grounding techniques. The following is an excellent visualization to center yourself, either in the morning or anytime throughout the day, especially when being negatively affected by people around you.

Centering Meditation

Once you have completed a few minutes of slow deep breathing, imagine that a soft, flexible green cord is attached to the base of your spine . . . Clearly observe this cord . . . The cord is slowly moving from your spine toward the floor . . . Imagine two more green cords that are attached to the soles of your feet . . . Now visualize all three green cords meeting at the Earth's surface and forming one large, strong green cord . . .

Observe the large green cord as gravity pulls the thick rope deeper toward the center of the Earth . . . The cable is now traveling through layers and layers of solid rock . . . deeper and deeper . . . You can clearly see the cord traveling as it slowly moves toward the center of the Earth . . .

Finally, the green cord arrives at the very center of the Earth . . . The rope anchors itself to the Earth's center, and you begin to slowly inhale calm, centered, and stable energy from the Earth's core . . . Visualize the energy slowly rising toward the Earth's surface with each inhalation . . .

The energy easily ascends towards the ground level . . .
Observe the grounding energy arrive at the Earth's surface . . .
The powerful energy ascends through the floor and into the
soles of your feet . . . You feel the energy rising up your legs . . .
You feel solid and centered, like a rock . . .

Now feel the Earth's energy enter the base of your spine
. . . The serene, grounded energy feels so soothing . . . Feel the
Earth's energy slowly travel up your spine through your lower
back . . . mid back . . . upper back . . . neck . . . all the way to
the top of your head . . .

You feel centered, calm, and strong as this core energy
circulates throughout your entire being . . . filling every cell of
your body . . . Breathe in the Earth's energy for a few moments
. . . You are calm, centered and happy . . . You are calm,
centered, and happy . . . You are calm, centered, and happy . . .

This grounding meditation is an excellent method to use prior to
dealing with a difficult situation. You may want to tape record this meditation until you can perform it from memory.

Another method to protect yourself from negative energy is to
visualize a white light surrounding you. This is an effective technique to
utilize before entering a room with a large group of people.

White Light Meditation

Once you have completed a few minutes of slow deep breathing
visualize a crystal-clear white light encircling your body . . .
Notice how the shimmering light encompasses every inch of
your skin . . . Observe clearly how strong the shield is . . .
Imagine negative energy bouncing off the impenetrable armor
and ricocheting back to its source . . . You are safe and
protected . . . You are safe and protected . . . You are safe and
protected . . .

Many students reported that when they practiced the white light
meditation before entering a stimulating situation, they were able to

remain calm. Try to remember to perform this brief meditation, which will give you much inner-peace.

A Restless Mind

When performing these meditative exercises, don't worry if you've spent some of a meditation session lost in thoughts. It's natural for seemingly random thoughts to constantly arise in the mind. To help cope with this stream of distractions you can use the Buddhist technique of simply witnessing your thoughts. When a distracting thought flits into your mind, simply acknowledge the thought and let it pass. Try to avoid engaging the thought—just observe that the mind is thinking, then let the thought go and return to your breath.

You may want to simply watch each thought as it arises. Each one is simply like a bus with a sign indicating a particular destination. As soon as you become aware of a thought, simply ask yourself if you want to go where that thought is taking you. Do you want to go to Angerville, ruminating about a recent hurtful experience? Do you want to travel on a bus going to Anxiety City, worrying about not being able to pay the bills? Instead, would you rather get on a bus traveling to Joy Town, as you return to watching your breathing and relaxing your muscles. You always have a choice about whether to remain a passenger on any of the stressful buses that are passing through your mind. You can always choose to disembark at any time from a negative mental journey.

Don't use the fact that you may have spent most of a meditation lost in thoughts as another reason to feel stress. I've been meditating daily for over twenty years, and I still frequently find myself lost in a myriad of thoughts. During some of my daily meditations I've pondered the great truths of life, such as "Is it better for me to eat hot cereal or eggs for breakfast?. . . If I have the eggs, I'll be getting more protein, but eggs have cholesterol . . . and then it will take longer to clean the pan. . . . Oh, I should have gotten gas at the cheaper station yesterday and saved ten cents a gallon . . . times ten gallons would be a dollar I would have saved . . . over a year that would be fifty two dollars . . . wow, thirty minutes are up already. . . . Oh yeah, let me repeat a mantra: peace, peace, peace."

The good news is that even if it appears that you've spent most of a meditation with a monkey mind jumping from branch to branch, you are still probably receiving benefits. The positive physiological effects of meditation have been validated by many scientific studies (Wallace 1970). One student told me that he felt that he wasn't focusing during one meditation, but when he answered the phone the caller asked if he was meditating since his voice sounded so tranquil. As you perform relaxation techniques regularly, deeper experiences of inner-peace will manifest in your life. Besides creating a peaceful mind, meditating will help you maintain a healthy body (Zeff 1981).

While meditation or progressive relaxation is an ideal way to center yourself in the morning, it's important to do whatever relaxation exercise nourishes your soul. You may find that praying, writing, or self-reflection has a soothing effect on your nervous system. Some HSPs prefer to start the day reading a spiritually uplifting book.

After your morning relaxation, it's important to eat a nourishing breakfast slowly and leave plenty of time for your commute to work. It's helpful to arise at the same time on weekends as you do during the week so that you'll be sleepy on Sunday evening and your sleep biorhythms will remain regular.

Creating an Evening Routine

While following a morning routine is very important for the highly sensitive person, your evening routine is another essential component that will help you become more tranquil. Since the quality of your sleep is affected by your evening routine, it is important to do calming activities in the evening. Your evening activities should consist of calming endeavors such as reading uplifting books, writing, taking a bath, or engaging in light discussions. About thirty minutes before going to bed, let go of the day by going inward. This is another good time for meditating or listening to a relaxation tape. By doing progressive relaxation, you will be able to release any stress that has accumulated during the day. In order to experience stage three and four of deep sleep (the level at which the immune system is activated), it helps to practice meditation and relaxation exercises throughout the day and especially at night, or the stress hormones that were released during the day may continue to be released while you're sleeping (Jacobs 1998).

If you spend the evening watching stimulating television shows, reading murder mysteries, or engaging in intense discussions, it will be more difficult to experience a good night's rest. If there's an arousing television show that you really want to watch, you can always record the show and watch it earlier on another day. It's important to save important or heavy discussions for the morning.

Victor, an HSP father of a teenage son, told me that he has learned that he must have quiet in the evening or he becomes too stimulated to fall asleep. Victor reported that his son, Chris, had borrowed his car one weekday night recently and that although the boy's curfew was 10 P.M. on weekdays, Chris didn't return home until after midnight. When the teenager finally returned, Victor's anger boiled over. He demanded the car keys and told Chris that he was going to discuss his future use of the car. Chris wisely responded that they should discuss the issue in the morning when they would both be calmer. However, Victor insisted on continuing a heated discussion, which increased his blood pressure, heart rate, and muscle tension, resulting in a sleepless night.

Paradoxically, when HSPs are in an out of balance state, they sometimes desire to be involved in activities that push them further off-center. Sometimes when you internalize the Type A lifestyle, you may actually enjoy watching overstimulating television shows or getting into intense discussions late at night, regardless of what they do to your sleep schedule. However, as you begin meditating and living a more contemplative life, you will instinctively begin to desire more peaceful activities.

HSPs are deeply affected by watching or reading about violence in the media. Watching violent, arousing shows may actually contribute to suppressing your immune system. As you identify with the anger you see on the screen or read about, stress chemicals called catecholamine and cortisone are released that can adversely affect your immune system. The effect of exposure to both anger and love on the immune system was shown in research by Harvard scientist David Mclelland, and later reproduced by the Heart Math Institute in California (Bhat 1995). Watching an anger-provoking movie suppressed the immune system (as measured by chemicals in the saliva) for five to six hours in study subjects. However, watching a movie about the compassionate work of Mother Teresa caused elevation of the immune level in the participants.

Since your senses have been exposed to stimulation throughout the day, it's important to try to spend some time in the evening in a quiet, dimly lit setting. When you really want to turn off the world in the evening, meditate or read with either earplugs or a headset in a quiet space. No matter how stressful the day has been, when you create a stimuli-free environment in the evening, you will be able to enter into a tranquil state.

In chapter 5 you'll learn many additional helpful hints for your evening routine that will help improve the quality of your sleep and the level of peace you have every day.

Creating a Daily Routine

- Your morning routine will set the tone for your day, while your evening routine will influence the quality of your sleep.

- Wake up fifteen to twenty minutes earlier than usual to begin your morning routine.

- Begin the day with some gentle stretching, yoga postures, or light calisthenics.

- Spend at least fifteen minutes in the morning centering yourself through meditation, progressive relaxation, or listening to a meditation tape.

- Eat a nourishing breakfast slowly.

- Leave plenty of time to commute to work.

- Your evening activities should consist of calming endeavors such as reading uplifting books, writing, meditating, taking a bath, or having light discussions.

- Try not to watch overstimulating or violent television shows in the evening.

- For thirty minutes prior to going to sleep, turn off the day and go inward by meditating, listening to a relaxation tape, or whatever helps you make the transition to a restful sleep.

—————————— *3* ——————————

Calm the Senses and Cope with Time Pressure

$\mathcal{I}$n the last chapter we discussed coping strategies to deal with our overstimulating Type A society. In this chapter we will discuss specific techniques for calming the senses and coping with time pressure. In order to survive in our overstimulating world we must diligently employ techniques to calm all five senses—hearing, touching, sight, taste, and smell. While we can't live free of stimuli, we can use specific tools to reduce the overstimulation of each of our senses.

Calming the Senses

An entire generation has now been brought up addicted to the overstimulation of the sense organs. As an example of the increased overstimulation in our electronic age, I've noticed that some amusement parks are creating full-sensory overload activities. New 4-D theaters are offering a frenetic visual experience, theater seats that buck and roll, and even the release of strange aromas. There may be a correlation between increased stimulation and the higher number of children diagnosed with hyperactive disorders. Unfortunately, the new panacea for hyperactive children is to medicate them with powerful drugs that may create innumerable side effects. However, if these same children lived in a natural environment without electronic devices, many of the "hyperactive" children would not need to be medicated (DeGrandpre 1999).

Hearing

Hearing is probably the sense that creates the most challenges for the HSP. If you happen to catch sight of something that causes negative stimulation, you can always close your eyes. However, it is much more difficult to tune out deleterious noises. With the advent of the now ubiquitous cell phones that ring everywhere, loud music blaring from powerful speakers, and honking from angry drivers, the sensitive person seems to be trapped in a cacophony of clamor. The cumulative effect of such grating sounds can create severe anxiety for the HSP.

To mask the jarring sounds of modern, urban life, you may want to play soft music in the background at home and at work. Listen to whatever type of music calms you down, from classical to jazz. If you don't like having soft music in the background, you may want to buy a white noise machine, which helps drown out startling noises by emitting a steady, soothing sound. The hum of a soothing fan, air conditioner, or air purifier also masks loud, erratic noises. An air purifier may soothe your nerves while cleaning indoor air pollution.

Whenever you stay in a motel or hotel you can reduce annoying city noise by turning on the air conditioner or fan. You can also take a small white noise machine with you when you travel if you don't want to rely on a fan or air conditioner. Please refer to chapter 5 for more information to help reduce noise to get a better night's sleep.

You can also periodically listen to a relaxation or a guided visualization tape or CD, which is quite efficacious for soothing your nerves. Many bookstores sell relaxation tapes and CDs or you can visit www.hspsurvival.com for more information. It's very helpful to take a headset with you when you venture out into the noisy world. You may want to carry an array of soothing tapes, including guided relaxation, classical music, or other spiritually uplifting sounds. Make sure that you take extra batteries with you so you're not stranded in a sea of sonic strife with no solution.

Another effective method to reduce noise is to wear earplugs. Some HSPs may find wearing earplugs uncomfortable, but if you can tolerate earplugs, it is a most effective means to mask irritating noises. Some people prefer wax earplugs, while others find the foam ones more comfortable. In extremely noisy situations you may want to wear earmuff-style headsets that construction workers use. These headsets cover the entire ear and some HSPs find them less intrusive than having to insert ear plugs. There are also noise-canceling headsets available that use sound waves to cancel out ambient noise. While these headsets offer clear music, they do not seem to mask noise any better than earplugs or earmuff-style headsets.

An audiologist can fit you for a custom made set of earplugs. The advantage of these specially constructed earplugs is that they will fit easily into your ear canal. When you really want to escape from the stimuli-saturated world, you can simply close your eyes and meditate wearing either earplugs, a regular headset, or an earmuff-style headset. In extremely noisy situations you can even wear earplugs while listening to your headset or wear an earmuff-style headset over earplugs.

Have you ever visited a recording studio? When the door to the studio is shut, you can't hear any outside noises. There are sound engineers who can help you soundproof your house or office, creating an HSP paradise of peace and tranquility. You may want to buy double-paned windows or heavy curtains to mask outside noises. Most importantly, the HSP has to be vigilant in finding quiet living and work environments. If you live in a noisy city, it's best that your home or office is facing a quiet backyard rather than a noisy street. When traveling, always ask the hotel or motel clerk for a quiet room on the top floor in the back.

Don't feel embarrassed using the techniques described in this section, such as wearing earplugs in public or requesting a quiet hotel room. Your main concern is taking good care of yourself to create inner peace.

What, me worry about noise? Not when I'm prepared!

Seeing

The reason that people meditate with their eyes closed is to shut out the stimuli from the outside world, allowing them to dive deeply into the peace that lies dormant within. By constantly receiving excessive stimuli through your eyes, you are directly overloading your nervous system and possibly creating anxiety and tension. Instead of staring endlessly at your television or your computer screen, which can overstimulate your nervous system, try an eye-opening idea—an eye-closing meditation break. Simply take a few moments while sitting at home or at work or even in your parked car to close your eyes and watch your breath. This mini-vacation can leave you feeling more peaceful and better able to deal with the stimuli.

It's deeply relaxing for HSPs to be able to look out a window at a beautiful nature scene. Take regular breaks throughout the day to really focus on the majestic tree in your back yard, the deep green grass of the front lawn, or the crystal-clear azure sky above. As you tune into the divine energy in nature, your anxiety level will decrease and your joy level will increase. If your living or work environment is saturated with artificial, urban stimuli, you can buy large pictures or posters of natural landscapes. You will feel so much better after gazing at a large picture of a mountain or an ocean scene. You may want to buy wallpaper of a lovely forest setting that makes you feel as if you are living in nature. Fill your home and office with plants and flowers to create a nurturing, positive environment.

Try to spend some time in nature every day, either walking or sitting in silence. Remember to stay focused in the present moment as you gaze at the magnificent array of luscious flowers or the cornucopia of cotton-candy clouds reflected in the shimmering water of a pond.

You may not consciously realize it, but some colors are more sooth-ing than others. It's important to surround yourself with calming colors such as white, blue, green, and other soft colors (Lad 1984). The colors in your house and office should be soothing for the nervous system. Bright shades of orange, yellow, and red can be overstimulating, ulti-mately increasing agitation for the HSP. Red is related to anger, which is so aptly exemplified by the expression "seeing red."

One day I noticed a client of mine driving up to my office in a bright red car, dressed in a flaming red suit, wearing fiery red lipstick, and sporting blazing orange hair. I needed to put on my sunglasses just to look at her! The client told me that she didn't understand why she was always angry and hot under the collar all the time. If she looked at the color of her collar, she would have understood what was making her feel so enraged. When you're out of balance, you may be attracted to the things that will push you even further out of balance, so surround your-self with soothing colors to create harmony in your life.

Many HSPs are sensitive to light. I've noticed that when I teach my day classes, I have frequent requests that I shut the blinds, since the bright sunlight can be quite distracting. HSPs don't have to sit in a dark-ened room, but it is important to adjust the lighting so it's not overstim-ulating you. It's a good idea to always carry a pair of sunglasses since you may have a challenging time going from soft indoor light into the bright sunlight.

It's best for the HSP not to be exposed to bright light late at night since it may not only interfere with falling asleep but may create too much stimulation for your nervous system. However, it is beneficial to expose yourself to light in the morning upon arising, which helps the neurotransmitters in the brain realize a new day has begun. Sometimes just a small amount of light seeping in under the bedroom door at night can disturb a sensitive person's sleep. You can always put a door sweep on the bottom of your door and seal any other openings. You may also want to buy some heavy drapes to seal out any bright light coming from streetlights or from a full moon. You can buy an eye mask that can filter out unwanted light. These masks can help you relax at times throughout the day as well as aid you in getting a good night's sleep.

Touching

One of the best ways an HSP (or non-HSP) can soothe tension is by receiving a gentle massage. However, some sensitive people may find that a massage is too invasive. It's crucial for you to constantly give feedback to the massage therapist as to the degree of pressure that feels comfortable. Due to your characteristic HSP openness, you may easily absorb the energy of the massage therapist, so be sure to interview the therapist before agreeing to a massage. Since some HSPs may not feel comfortable being touched by strangers, they may benefit more from receiving a massage from a partner or a close friend.

You may not even have to go to a spa or body-work studio to get your massage. Some stores, such as those specializing in health products, now employ massage therapists. You deserve to take a ten-minute break now and then for a back and shoulder massage. If you can't afford regular massages, you may want to take a massage class with your partner and trade massages. Another excellent option is to massage yourself in the early evening to release the stress of the day.

Warm, organic sesame oil is the only oil that soaks into all seven tissue layers and deeply calms down the nervous system. Sesame oil is used extensively in Ayurveda, the ancient healing science from India. According to Ayurveda, the properties in some oils can have a cooling or heating effect on people. Since sesame oil is the most heating oil, don't use it when you feel overheated or on a hot summer day. When it's hot outside, try massaging yourself with cooling coconut oil. Don't buy the toasted sesame oil that is used for Chinese cooking or you'll end up smelling like a wok (which could really stir fry your nerves). You can purchase organic sesame oil at your local health-food store.

Heat up three or four ounces of the oil and massage yourself gently and slowly throughout your entire body, from your head to your toes. Let the oil remain on your body for about ten minutes, then shower. Do not put oil on the soles of your feet or you could slip. If you don't want to do a full-body massage simply gently apply some warm sesame oil to your forehead and ears. You can also purchase sesame oil that has been medicated with calming herbs for really deep relaxation (for medicated oils visit www.oilbath.com). Apply the medicated sesame oil to your fore-head and ears in the evening and watch your tension float away.

Warm water is very healing and nurturing for your body. Taking a warm bath can be a wonderfully relaxing treat, especially when you add a few drops of essential oil of lavender. Adding any calming essential oils can be deeply soothing for your nervous system. Sitting in a hot tub with the jets shooting warm water on your tense muscles for just ten minutes is another effective treatment to instantly calm the body. You may want to purchase a massage showerhead for your shower and stand under-neath the soothing stream for some time.

Make sure that you have a comfortable chair to sit on at home and at work. Many stores sell massage cushions that fit on your chair. You can also buy an electric hand-held massage wand. Many people suffer from back pain from sleeping on a bed that is too soft or too hard. Make sure that your bed suits your particular constitution so that your muscles are relaxed throughout the night.

Touch itself is very healing. Research indicates that infants who are touched are emotionally and physically healthier than those babies who are deprived of touch (Field 2000). Make sure that you get plenty of hugs every day. The late spiritual teacher Leo Busgalia used to tell his audiences that everyone needs at least five hugs a day. Have you met your quota for nourishing hugs today?

Ammachi, the spiritual teacher from India, is known internationally as the hugging saint. She travels around the world embracing thousands of people daily and has hugged over twenty million people. People line up for hours to receive a hug from Amma because the unconditional love from her touch is so healing. According to Deepak Chopra, "Amamchi is the embodiment of pure love, and her presence heals" (Amritaswarup-ananda 1994). When we are held and nurtured by another from a place of unconditional love, we are instantaneously uplifted.

However, If you don't like being held tightly or even gently embraced, please don't feel like you should be hugged. Since HSPs star-tle easily, tell your partner, relatives, and friends that you don't like someone surprising you with an unexpected embrace. One HSP men-tioned that it really disturbs him when his wife startles him by hugging him from behind when he is washing the dishes.

Smelling

Many HSPs are sensitive to odors. Some of my HSP students have reported that whenever they are near anyone who has on perfume, they become nauseated. If you're sensitive to these kinds of synthetic odors and find yourself on a plane or in a theater sitting near someone who is wearing perfume, it's best to immediately move your seat. There may actually be a correlation between chemical sensitivity and being an HSP.

If you have an adverse reaction to odors, you need to make sure that your house is free of any noxious fumes. It's also important not to work in a facility that is permeated with unhealthy odors. There are many natural cleaning products available at your local health-food store that you can suggest be used by the custodians at your office. Buying an air purifier can minimize indoor pollution and sanitize the air. It can also mask jarring noises.

With increased pollution, more people are wearing masks in public to avoid inhaling unhealthy, noxious odors. If you decide to wear a mask, make sure that you purchase a high quality model. Many people wear masks in polluted environments. For example, when I visited large cities in India and Mexico I wore a mask, and even though some local people may have thought it looked strange, I was protected from inhaling noxious odors.

One of the benefits of HSPs having a keen sense of smell is the ability to use this sense to aid in calming down your nervous system. Aromatherapy is a branch of herbal medicine that uses the inhalation of essential oils extracted from plants and herbs. Many wonderfully scented essential oils, like lavender or rose can be effective against stress. Larger health-food stores will be able to guide you in how to use these scents. But, although aromatherapy can be an excellent approach to calm your nervous system, some HSPs may have an adverse reaction to it. Before you go out and buy a potpourri pot and essential oils you may want to test the procedure by taking a light sniff of the oils to determine if this is an appropriate therapy for you.

If you can tolerate the aromas, you might use lavender, jasmine, and rose, which can alter the brain waves to produce calmness and relaxation. Some businesses are beginning to utilize aromatherapy since management has discovered that calming fragrances help employees work more efficiently throughout the day (Worwood 1997). You can also burn some incense of sandalwood or rose, which can have a calming effect on the nervous system. You may also want to consider purchasing a pillow filled with calming herbs, which promotes relaxation as you inhale during sleep (www.sonomalavender.com).

Make sure that you have good airflow at home and at work. Check the filters on your air conditioning, heating units, and air purifiers regularly. If you live on a quiet street, you may want to open your windows to release stale odors.

Eating and Drinking

Some HSPs are sensitive to hot or cold food and beverages. It's generally better to consume warm drinks and foods rather than those that are piping hot. According to the healing system of Ayurveda, eating warm foods can calm your nervous system (Lad 1984). I had one student who had severe anxiety for several years. She mentioned that she had been on a raw food diet during the time she experienced increased tension. As we investigated her situation, we discovered a correlation between her anxiety and her cold, raw food diet. She reported a few months later that her anxiety level had dramatically decreased when she began eating warm, cooked foods.

Another HSP reported that when he tried eating just fruit for breakfast in the winter he became very nervous. When he switched to hot cereal he felt calmer and more grounded. You may want to avoid drinking ice water, since the cold can be a shock to the nervous system and lower your digestive fire. Whenever you go out to eat at a restaurant, you can ask for water with no ice. Drinking iced water on a freezing winter day can increase anxiety and nervousness.

However, in the summer if you're feeling overheated and want to cool down, it's okay to drink cold water as long as you do not have an adverse reaction (like a headache). Another option for cooling the body is to drink water with a little lime juice squeezed into it. You may sometimes have difficulty consuming frozen foods such as ice cream. Ice-cold frozen desserts can sometimes cause headaches in sensitive people, so it's best to let any frozen treat melt in your mouth slowly.

Drinking some warm milk can be an excellent relaxant for you. It's important to drink lots of pure water daily to flush your system of toxins. Drinking a cup of calming herb tea, such as chamomile, can calm the nervous system. Try to buy fresh chamomile at a health food store and let the herbs steep in boiling water for five minutes, then strain. This medicinal libation is more potent than simply using a chamomile tea bag. Minimizing the use of caffeine such as coffee, black tea, and soft drinks may reduce your anxiety. Many of my students have been successful slowly reducing their intake of coffee through a gradual process. I recommend that each day you put a little more milk or soy milk in your coffee, so that in a month your cup of coffee will be only 25 percent coffee and 75 percent milk. The decrease in caffeine can help you feel more peaceful throughout the day.

While some people find drinking alcohol relaxing, other highly sensitive people actually have an adverse reaction to even one alcoholic drink. Even if you think it's "no big deal" to drink a glass of wine at dinner, it's important to know your body's reactions to alcohol and not just go along with the crowd.

The good news is that your sensitivity to taste gives you a huge capacity to really enjoy delicious meals. Another benefit of being an HSP is that your sensitive taste buds help you discover if a food is rancid, so you won't eat contaminated food. One HSP had such a strong sense of taste that she actually worked as a wine taster. Maybe you can obtain a job tasting chocolate. For many people, a job like that could be considered quite a benefit of having sensitive taste buds.

Take a Mini Retreat Twice a Week

Since you are sensitive to stimuli and are easily overwhelmed, it's important that you give yourself a break by taking a mini retreat at least twice a week. It is your birthright to experience inner peace and joy. So make sure that you set time aside specifically for relaxation. You can set aside a few hours one day during the week and a few hours on the weekend for nurturing yourself. It may initially feel like a luxury to spend four hours a week calming your nervous system, but in my opinion it's a necessity for the highly sensitive person. If you needed some regular special medical treatment such as dialysis, you wouldn't think twice about going to the doctor regularly to maintain your health. Likewise, the mini retreat is essential for HSPs to function in this overstimulating world. During your mini retreat you will be nourishing your body, emotions, and soul.

Inform your family or housemates that you need some quiet time when you won't be disturbed. If this isn't possible in your home, try to find another place to nurture yourself. Do you have a friend, relative, or coworker who would be willing to offer their home to you for a few hours during the week? Perhaps you could offer to cook, clean, or take care of your "retreat landlord's" plants and pets as a trade.

The first step in creating your mini retreat is to turn off all the phones and other electronic equipment, and make sure that you are not disturbed by any outside stimuli, especially members of your household. If it's difficult to create a silent environment, create a noise-free atmosphere by playing some calming music, turning on a white noise machine, or wearing earplugs. Now's the time to just relax in bed or on your couch and read that spiritually uplifting book you never seem to get to.

If you feel sleepy while reading take a no-guilt refreshing nap. If you enjoy aromatherapy, put some calming essential oils in a potpourri pot or burn some incense. If you're thirsty, make a cup of chamomile tea or your favorite relaxing beverage. Prepare a special healthy snack (preferably without sugar) and spend some time really noticing the taste of each scrumptious morsel that you eat. Try closing your eyes and concentrating on the delicious taste on your tongue.

Next, try practicing some spiritually uplifting exercise such as hatha yoga or tai chi. You may want to purchase a yoga or tai chi DVD or videotape. Another option is to just do some gentle stretching or go for a walk in nature. After performing some gentle exercise you may want to engage in any of the following: meditate, listen to a relaxation tape, do progressive relaxation, pray, read something spiritual uplifting, or do some journal writing.

Finally, you may want to massage your body with warm sesame oil followed by a warm bath. Add anything you like to the bath, from lavender oil to Epsom salts. Spend as much time as you want massaging and bathing yourself. Don't set up a rigid schedule to follow, but intuitively partake in the various relaxing techniques described above that calm down your nervous system. You may want to spend the entire time during your mini retreat partaking in just one activity.

You deserve to enjoy regular mini retreats, so right now begin penciling in dates on your calendar for your nurturing sessions. However, check in with yourself so you don't start feeling overwhelmed by yet another thing on your calendar. I also recommend taking longer, full day or weekend retreats once or twice a year. You can spend some time in a cabin in the woods or anywhere where you can have a few days of real peace.

Coping with Time Pressure

As an HSP, you will probably find it challenging when you're under time pressure. Combined with your high sense of responsibility, functioning under time constraints can be one of the most difficult aspects of being a highly sensitive person. In this section you will learn specific techniques to successfully deal with the daily pressures of our fast-paced modern society.

Driving

The term "a relaxing drive" may be considered an oxymoron, given our congested urban roads. I used to regularly drive on overcrowded freeways and consequently became conditioned to sitting in traffic listening to honking drivers exhibit road rage. However, when I lived in the rural Sierra mountains in California, driving actually became a calming activity. Due to a series of events, I needed to relocate to the San Francisco Bay Area, and I felt like a country bumpkin as I was overwhelmed by all the stimulation in the densely populated megalopolis. Soon after relocating, I had an important job interview at 5 P.M. on a weekday in a city located fifteen miles from my home. I naively figured that it would take thirty minutes to arrive at my destination, since most of the driving would be on a freeway. To my utter shock and dismay, I was stuck on a freeway that was clogged with cars slowly traveling in bumper-to-bumper traffic for over an hour. I fumed with anger as my anxiety level and blood pressure rose. I realized that I would be very late for my interview. Ironically, I was interviewing for a job teaching stress-reduction!

Try to avoid driving on the freeways during rush hour. If you must attend a meeting that coincides with a peak traffic hour, either use your city's mass transit system or arrive in the area several hours earlier and spend the extra time taking a walk in nature or meditating.

Since HSPs are conscientious about everything, including tardiness, it's important to leave early for your destination in case there are unexpected traffic jams. Worrying about being late to an appointment can really increase your anxiety level. If you're going to be late, either call the person you're meeting or just try to accept the situation. I recommend not wearing a watch so you won't further upset yourself by checking to see how late you are. You may want to cover your car clock with a beautiful picture so that you're glancing at tranquility instead of a cue for anxiety. You can always move the picture if you really need to obtain the correct time.

With the increase of road rage, urban highways have turned into a stress-inducing nightmare for the HSP. The best way to avoid angry drivers is not to interact with them. It may be more relaxing to drive in the slow lane and let all the harried drivers pass you by. However, some of my HSP students have told me that they feel uncomfortable driving in the slow lane. I feel that this may be due to their having internalized the values of our fast-paced society. When you're rushing to an appointment, driving in the fast lane, you may become overwhelmed and out of balance. Driving in the slow lane is a great way to learn how to downshift your consciousness from the mores of our time-urgent society.

You will find it more relaxing to listen to a calming tape or classical music while you're driving rather than news of the latest murder or terrorist attack on the radio. The proliferation of negative yet addictive talk show hosts who promote both stimulating and vengeful banter may be anathema to a calm nervous system. The term "hate radio" has been coined to illustrate the hostility and rage that is broadcast from some radio stations. When you drive in the slow lane listening to pleasant music, you are able to transcend the stimuli-saturated world. But, don't listen to a deep-relaxation tape, since it can make you dangerously sleepy while driving.

Contrary to the belief of most drivers, a yellow traffic light does not mean to speed up through the intersection. Try to view a red light as an opportunity to spend a few minutes relaxing the muscles in your body and doing some slow abdominal breathing. If there is a traffic jam and your car is at a standstill, you can also use this occasion to relax more and more deeply as the other drivers become more and more anxious.

If you find yourself sitting in a sluggish traffic jam, you might try some relaxation techniques to calm down. Although the following story is not about driving, I think Cynthia's experience of using deep breathing and repeating a mantra could help you in your next traffic snarl. Cynthia found herself waiting in a long bank line. The customers became angry as the line came to a standstill. At first she also started complaining about the incompetent tellers and the poor management of the bank. The other people who were waiting in line enjoyed listening to her derogatory comments—misery loves company. After some time, Cynthia decided to do slow abdominal breathing. She mentally repeated the word "peace." When it was finally her turn at the teller's station, she felt relaxed and happy, while the other customers were still livid with rage. The next time you find yourself waiting in bumper-to-bumper traffic or in a long line, try going inward by repeating a mantra and doing slow abdominal breathing, then notice how serene you feel.

Walking

In this fast-paced society most people have become habituated to walking rapidly. When I lived in the rural Sierra mountains, I had a neighbor who had been a stockbroker in New York. Although he had lived in the tranquil environment for many years, I remember frequently observing him striding hurriedly on a forested dirt road, constantly looking at his watch. Sometimes you can take the stockbroker out of Wall Street but you can't take Wall Street out of the stockbroker.

One of the easiest and least expensive methods to reduce stimuli for the HSP is to take a walk in nature every day. While strolling amongst natural beauty, you may want to practice a walking meditation. It's important to stay focused in the present moment when you are walking in nature rather than transforming the hike into an intense business meeting between you and yourself.

As you walk, try moving as slowly as possible and becoming aware of your movements as you place one foot leisurely in front of the other. Be aware as your heel and toe touch the ground and as you pick up your back foot. Another technique is to simply take note of what you are hearing. Listen to the sweet songs of the birds, the flowing of a waterfall, or a squirrel scampering up a tree. Next, just observe what you are seeing. Gaze deeply at the cornucopia of multicolored flowers, the crystal-clear blue sky, or the velvety green grass. Next, become aware of what you are touching. Your shoes contact the soft ground and your arms gently stroke your coat as they sway back and forth. Go ahead and enjoy these tactile sensations. Finally, just notice the activity of walking. You can become aware of your walking by repeating the words "walking, walking" silently to yourself. Then repeat in your mind "hearing, hearing," "seeing, seeing," and "touching, touching" (Hanh 1991). You have now turned your walk in nature into a blissful meditation.

Buddhist teacher Thich Nhat Hanh teaches another wonderful walking meditation that can help you remain in the present (1991). Instead of ruminating over the past or worrying about the future, repeat a mantra with each step. You may choose as your mantra "I have arrived" as you put your right foot down and "I am home" as your left foot falls. You are safe at home with every step you take. You could also mentally repeat the mantra "peace" or "calm" with each step. Walking meditation is an excellent practice for the highly sensitive person because it exercises the body while relaxing the mind.

Talking

Talking is probably one of the most overstimulating activities that the HSP has to contend with. I have noticed that people that I've met from the Nordic countries tend to talk less, which may be one of the reasons why those societies are inclined to be peaceful. In our Type A culture, people frequently equate verbosity with control and success. However, when you become involved in a rapid-fire discussion, it can be quite jarring to your sensitive nervous system.

One of the most effective methods to reduce stimulation and create inner peace is by spending time in silence. When you're in silence in the presence of other people, you don't have to constantly give your opinion or defend yourself. You can just relax and simply observe people projecting their beliefs, which actually becomes a meditative experience. You can tell people that being in silence helps calm your nervous system, releasing you from the expectation of needing to be engaged in intense verbal interactions. When your family and friends notice how much more peaceful you have become, they may want to emulate your quiet behavior.

It can be quite stressful for the HSP to respond quickly while conversing, since we generally like to process information slowly. A technique that I have found very effective for reducing stimulation in intense conversations is the "pause for five seconds" technique. Both people agree to wait just five seconds before responding to the other person. For instance, say that your spouse tells you that you're running late getting ready for an outing and you may curtly respond that you are not late. The stage is set for an overstimulating quarrel as both parties respond quickly and defensively. Now try a new scenario of waiting five seconds before responding to the same statement. Wait and count in your head 1 . . . 2 . . . 3 . . . 4 . . . 5. Your new response will probably be that you just need a few more minutes. By utilizing this approach, an intense argument can be transformed into a calm interaction.

If you tend to talk rapidly, ask your family, friends, and coworkers to remind you to speak slower. You may want to try an experiment. Observe how you feel after talking rapidly. Are your muscles tense? Is your breathing shallow? Do you feel nervous? Next, spend some time talking very slowly and observe how your body and emotions feel. While HSPs like to process information slowly, they are frequently pushed into a quick response by the majority culture.

Try practicing being in silence for short periods of time each day while in the presence of family and friends. At first it may feel uncomfortable, but as you begin to enjoy the peace and quiet, you will want to be in silence more. However, if you are already a quiet or shy person, don't use being in silence as an excuse to avoid interacting with people. We need to create a balance between our verbal interactions and quiet time. When students have told me that it drives them crazy to talk slowly or listen to people who talk slowly, it's just an example of how far away from being in a balanced and relaxed state they are. When we are not in a harmonious state, we crave the things that will make us feel even more off-center like incessant, rapid talking.

Dining

In chapter 2 on techniques to reduce overstimulation, we discussed how important it is to include a nourishing, slowly eaten breakfast in your morning routine. One of my students suffered from chronic indigestion. When I examined his eating habits, he told me that for breakfast he just hurriedly drank a cup of coffee and ate a donut at the office, for lunch he ate a sandwich while working at his desk, and for dinner he stopped by a fast food restaurant for a quick meal. How could he not suffer from indigestion with such a poor diet? However, even if you eat only the healthiest organic vegetables, fruits, and whole grains, you still may get indigestion if you eat your meal too quickly.

The more mindfully you eat, the easier the food can be digested and the more you can reduce over-arousal. When you're really aware of the food that you are eating, you will naturally feel more peaceful. Have you ever experienced the following scenario? You have gone to a fancy restaurant and spent a lot of money on a delicious, gourmet meal. Just as you were putting the last bite of food into your mouth, you suddenly realized that you were so engrossed in the intense conversation you'd been having that you were totally unaware of the meal that you'd been eating. Try being aware of really tasting your food during every meal. You may want to try eating in silence or with just minimal, light, and pleasant conversation.

Mindful eating is a challenging new habit to develop, especially for adults who were raised to eat while watching television or while always involved in intense conversations during mealtime. Why not experiment by trying mindful eating for just one meal a week, and observe how you feel at the end of the meal. Try focusing on the food that you are eating without engaging in any other stimulating activity (reading, watching television, surfing the Internet, talking, etc.). Pretend that you are a restaurant critic concentrating on the quality of the food that you are ingesting. Notice how much more you enjoy the meal and observe how relaxed you feel after eating.

Writing

Contrary to public opinion, they don't teach bad penmanship to doctors in medical school. The reason you may have difficulty reading a doctor's prescription is due to the physician's time-urgent behavior. With the advent of the computer, most people do not do as much writing by hand. However, it's still beneficial to monitor your handwriting to reduce stimulation. I remember when I was studying with Dr. Ray Rosenman, author of *Type A Behavior and Your Heart* (1974), a classmate and I were working in dyads to determine each other's personality type. I was talking very slowly, and my partner told Dr. Rosenman that he thought I was a Type B personality. However, Dr. Rosenman asked me to write a sentence and as he showed my sloppy penmanship to the class, he stated that I was a Type A.

Learn to monitor your handwriting by trying the following exercise. After writing very quickly for a few minutes, close your eyes and see how you feel. Notice if you are holding the pen tightly. Is your breathing shallow or do your shoulders feel tight? You can also try this experiment while typing quickly on the keyboard. Now consciously write or type very slowly and notice how much more relaxed your body feels. If your handwriting is so poor that you can't even read it, make yourself rewrite the sentence slowly, enjoying the clear handwriting and a new sense of inner-peace.

Telephoning

The ubiquitous telephone is an important source of overarousal for the HSP. With the advent of cell phones, the stimulation can now be overwhelming. How do you think it affects your nervous system when you are driving on a freeway at sixty-five miles per hour, holding the steering wheel with one hand and your cell phone with the other? I recommend that you turn off your cell phone when you are driving. The predominance of cell phones is another symptom of our overstimulating, addictive world. Most HSPs find it extremely agitating to be forced to listen to other people's private discussions while shopping in a store, waiting in a bank line, or walking down the street. Have you noticed when you're in an airport lounge waiting for your plane to take off that there are many people sitting near you talking loudly into their cell phones. To deal with this bombardment of stimuli, you can listen to soothing music on your headset or wear earplugs. What ever happened to phone booths or proper phone etiquette? Perhaps HSPs can help create some cell-phone-free zones the way we helped create no smoking areas. However, some positive aspects of owning a cell phone are that HSPs can receive instant support from others and feel more secure, especially in emergency situations. As previously mentioned, to cope with the cacophony of intrusive noise, never leave home without a headset or ear plugs.

Instead of hearing the ringing of your phone as another negative stimulus in your life, transform the sound into a relaxation cue. Just as if you were a member of a retreat being called to meditation with the sound of a bell, let the ringing be a reminder for you to practice deep relaxation (Hanh 1991).

Try not to answer the phone until the third or fourth ring (Hanh 1991). Use those few moments to relax all your muscles while you take a few slow, deep breaths, and mentally repeat a mantra such as "calm" or "peace." So, when you're feeling overwhelmed, instead of answering the phone with a curt, irritated hello, you'll answer the phone in a very slow, relaxed voice. This is an easy practice to integrate into your life. Also, since HSPs startle easily, it may be a good idea to lower the volume on your phone.

Using the Computer

It's incredible that the Internet has been functioning for fewer than ten years since it is now such an integral part of society. Virtually all of your friends and colleagues have e-mail addresses. People frequently may ask you for your e-mail address rather than your phone number. When was the last time that you received a handwritten or even typed letter from a friend by mail? The overstimulating Internet and computer have become the foundation of life in the twenty-first century.

The HSP must use discrimination regarding computer usage. Many people will have to spend much of their workday sitting in front of a computer. Try to take breaks every fifteen minutes for stretching or a short walking meditation. If this is not practical, you can simply close your eyes and watch your breath for a few moments. But you should take regular breaks from your computer to avoid developing back, neck, and wrist pain. In addition to potential physical ailments, computer over-use can create eyestrain, nervousness, and a feeling of being overwhelmed as you are bombarded by stimuli.

After work it's important to limit your use on the computer. To minimize feeling overwhelmed when checking your e-mail messages, only open those that are from someone you know, install a spam filter, and don't give your e-mail address out to many people. In your desire to be conscientious, you may tend to respond to every insignificant e-mail request. But if you don't limit your time on the computer, you can get lost in a cyber world of overarousal, clicking deeper and deeper into a neverending search that will aggravate your nervous system. You may want to set a timer in another room that will motivate you to leave your computer so that you will be able to stop and reflect on what you have been doing. Spending life in a virtual Internet reality can create nervousness, tension, and insomnia.

You've been reading for long enough. Go ahead, get up, and go for a walking meditation. Enjoy, enjoy, enjoy!

Using the Senses to Calm the HSP

- Avoid jarring noises by listening to relaxing background music or wearing earplugs.

- Give yourself or receive a massage on a regular basis.

- Reduce the time you sit in front of a television or computer screen and gaze at beautiful pictures or nature frequently.

- Reduce your use of caffeine by drinking calming herbal teas and a lot of pure water instead of coffee, black tea, or soda.

- Eat warm, nurturing food.

- Try inhaling the scents of calming essential oils or incense.

- Take a mini retreat twice a week and a longer retreat several times a year.

Important Points in Reducing
Time Pressure

- Listen to soothing music while driving slowly.

- Try to avoid driving during peak traffic hours.

- Utilize the opportunity of red lights and traffic jams as cues to spend time practicing relaxation techniques.

- Regularly practice slow, walking meditations in nature to stay calm and focused in the present.

- Try talking more slowly and being in silence sometimes.

- To reduce overstimulating arguments, wait five seconds before responding during an intense conversation.

- Try mindful eating during at least one meal a week without engaging in any other stimuli such as reading, watching television, or talking.

- Try writing and typing at a slower rate.

- Transform the ring of the telephone into a relaxation cue by not answering the phone until the third or fourth ring, if possible, while using the precious moments to relax deeply.

- Minimize your use of the computer, phones, and television.

———————— *4* ————————

Maintaining a
Healthy Body

𝒥n the last chapter we learned specific techniques to help us stay centered emotionally. This chapter will offer information and techniques on how to maintain a healthy body. According to Kenneth Pelletier, internationally known specialist in stress reduction, between 50 to 80 percent of all diseases have stress-related origins (1977). Since the HSP is more vulnerable to stress and feeling overwhelmed than the non-HSP, it's important for you to maintain a preventative health-maintenance program. In my interviews with HSPs, I found that 98 percent of the respondents stated that stress at work has adversely affected their physical or emotional health.

Regardless of the strength of their immune system, highly sensitive people tend to experience illness more deeply and find themselves more upset when they are sick than non-HSPs. The HSP also has a lower threshold for pain than the non-HSP, making you more aware of illness in your body.

Stress can contribute to a compromised immune system making you more susceptible to contracting both viral and bacterial infections (Goldberg 1993). Several HSPs reported that they noticed a direct correlation between their stress level and the number of colds that they experience. Many have reported that they have improved their immune system through diet, exercise, vitamins, and minerals as well as other supplements. If you have a stressed immune system you could employ the following practical measures to boost your immune function. Try increasing your intake of fruits and vegetables while abstaining from foods that lower the immune system, like sugar, maintaining an appropriate exercise program, taking herbs and supplements, and keeping warm in the winter and avoiding exposure to contagious people.

A Healthy Diet for the HSP

As an HSP, it's important for you to be careful about your diet. Certain foods can actually increase tension and anxiety. Other foods may compromise your immune system. When you use discrimination about which foods you eat, you will function at an optimal level.

Things to Be Aware of When Improving your Diet

The following are items to be careful about when shopping, cooking, and eating:

- ✂ **Food allergies:** Some highly sensitive people may have more food allergies than non-HSPs. Therefore, it's important to thoroughly read the ingredients listed on food labels and visit an allergist if you suspect food allergies.

- ✂ **Processed foods:** Many processed foods contain potentially harmful ingredients such as carcinogenic dyes, MSG (monosodium glutamate), excessive amounts of salt and sugar, and polyunsaturated fat. Foods that are high in sugar and refined carbohydrates with a high glycemic count may cause a burst of energy or hyperactivity followed by depression or anxiety.

- ✄ **High glycemic count:** The glycemic index measures the degree your blood sugar increases in the two to three hours after eating carbohydrates that are quickly broken down (Whitaker 2001). Products containing white flour, most processed cereals, and white potatoes (not sweet potatoes) are examples of foods with a high glycemic count. For the glycemic index of various foods, visit the web site www.mendosa.com.

- ✄ **Spicy foods:** May create a stimulating reaction for some sensitive people.

- ✄ **Items labeled "all natural" or "low fat":** Many of the major food companies are trying to cash in on the healthy diet trend, and occasionally you may find unhealthy ingredients such as refined sugar and preservatives in some "health foods."

- ✄ **Fast-food restaurants:** Try to stay away from fast-food restaurants that tend to sell food containing high levels of sugar, salt, fat, and chemicals.

- ✄ **Commercially grown fruits and vegetables:** Be careful about ingesting pesticides found on commercially grown fruits and vegetables.

Creating a Healthy Diet

Since you are constantly bombarded by advertisements that encourage you to buy unhealthy food, you need to get support from family and friends for developing new, healthy dietary habits. You may want to read books about the importance of a healthy diet and shop at health-food stores.

There are literally hundreds of diet books on the market. This can be overwhelming for the HSP trying to choose the right one. However, if you follow the general guidelines of eating less processed food, sugar, salt, and preservatives while increasing your consumption of organic veggies, fruits, and whole grains, you are likely to improve your immune system and reduce anxiety.

Sometimes when your body is out of balance you may crave foods that make you more out of balance. For example, the more that you eat foods saturated with salt and sugar, the more you will tend to desire them. Movie theater concessions sometimes sell popcorn laden with salt so customers will buy sugary soft drinks.

One student, Jean, told the class that she was addicted to eating chocolate candy every afternoon. However, as a New Year's resolution, she decided to abstain from sugar for a period of several months. When Jean finally ate her first sweet after the sugar fast, the candy actually tasted bitter to her and she could no longer consume the sugary treat. The more you eat calming, natural foods, the more you will crave them.

It would be beneficial to increase your intake of organic veggies, fruits, and whole grains. Although organic produce is slightly more expensive, the few extra dollars a week that you'll spend to avoid ingesting food sprayed with pesticides could prove to be very cost effective in terms of your long-term health.

When beginning a new diet you need to be gentle with yourself. For example, little by little you can reduce processed foods as you increase organic vegetables, fruit, and whole grains in your diet. The key to your new healthy diet should be moderation.

It's also important not to overeat. If you leave half of the stomach empty, the body will digest the food properly, avoiding indigestion and tension. You may be increasing the workload of your heart when you overeat, ultimately creating more stress. Eat to live; do not live to eat (Amritaswarupananda 1989). You may want to try fasting for just one day if it's not cold outside. However, it's generally not beneficial for the HSP to do long fasts since your sensitivity may create adverse emotional and physiological reactions if you deprive yourself of food for many days.

In Western countries we are blessed to have a cornucopia of tasty foods available. However, as mentioned in chapter 3 on calming the senses, while we have so much delicious food available, most people usually don't take the time to really enjoy a meal. Remember to take the time to eat slowly in a peaceful environment.

Although many people are reducing their consumption of red meat, a nonvegetarian diet could be healthier than a vegetarian diet that includes a pint of ice cream a day. Also, it's better to be a nonjudgmental meat eater than a judgmental vegetarian who condemns people who eat red meat. Since every constitution is different, experiment to find the diet that can help you stay healthy. If you experience flatulence, excessive stomach acidity, constipation, or diarrhea, you may want to consult your physician or a nutritionist to make changes in your diet.

According to Ayurveda, eating foods that are heavy, warm, and moist helps promote calmness for the vata constitution, which tends to have a sensitive nervous system (Frawley 1989). Eating foods such as warm soup, casseroles, and hot cereal are both nurturing and calming, especially in the winter. You may want to buy the book *Ayurvedic Cooking for Westerners* by Amadea Morningstar and follow the diet for the vata constitution. Heavy, warm, and moist foods are excellent for giving the inner-nourishment that the HSP needs. I recommend eating more cooked vegetables in the winter and more salads in the summer.

Eating complex carbohydrates can increase serotonin, a brain neurotransmitter that is calming to the nervous system. However, foods high in protein may block the synthesis of serotonin, making you feel more alert. These effects were demonstrated in a study in which people reported feeling more alert following a high protein lunch and sleepier following a high-carbohydrate lunch (Jacobs 1998).

Between meals, you may want to eat a healthy snack such as fruit, veggies, nonfat yogurt, nuts, or seeds. Did you know that if you eat celery sticks you actually lose weight since it takes more calories to chew the celery than there is in the vegetable? Try a delicious snack that satisfies your sweet tooth by cutting up an apple and banana (or any fruit) and top them with one tablespoon of natural (sugar-free) berry syrup or jam and shredded coconut. Try not to have sugary, processed foods in the house to avoid temptation, and stock your kitchen with healthy, natural foods.

A Sample Diet for the HSP

Since each HSP is unique, follow the diet that helps you feel calm and maintains your optimal health. I have listed below a few sample meals that are both calming and healthy for the HSP.

Breakfast Suggestions

1. Oatmeal, oat bran, or rice bran (which has a very low glycemic index) topped with nonfat plain yogurt, milk, or soy milk. You may also want to put some cinnamon on your cereal and use the herb stevia as a sweetener, which may help to control blood sugar.

2. Sprouted bread with salt-free butter, sugar-free jam, or soy or low fat cheese.

3. Eggs cooked in olive oil cooking spray.

Lunch Suggestions

1. A large portion of lightly steamed or lightly sautéed vegetables and/or salad with tuna, salmon, sardines, lean turkey, or chicken and sprouted bread. Top off your cooked veggies with olive oil, low-salt soy sauce, or some nonfat yogurt, then garnish with sesame or sunflower seeds and nuts.

2. Vegetable bean soup, cooked veggies, or salad and sprouted bread.

Dinner Suggestions

1. A large portion of lightly steamed or lightly sautéed vegetables and/or salad, whole grains, fish, lean chicken, or turkey.

2. A casserole, vegetable bean soup, or your favorite healthy dish served with cooked veggies or salad and sprouted bread.

When cooking your vegetables, steam them for only two to three minutes so that they are still crunchy and have not lost their vitamins or enzymes. If you stir-fry your vegetables, you may want to use olive oil or olive oil cooking spray in a nonstick pan. Shop at your local health food store and buy a huge selection of colorful organic veggies. When eating a fattening main dish, try consuming only half of the normal serving, and eat the heavier foods very slowly, savoring the taste of each morsel. If you like fish, it's best to eat seafood that is high in omega 3 oils and low in mercury such as salmon and sardines. Please note that due to high levels of mercury the Federal Drug Administration advises women of child-bearing age to avoid shark, swordfish, and king mackerel (2003). It's best to eat fruit between meals or two hours after eating a large meal since fruit does not digest well combined with other foods.

As I mentioned before, there are many different diets out there, and you need to follow the one that works for you. Go to your library or local bookstore to obtain many appetizing, healthy, natural recipes. Try to be aware if the food you eat calms you down or makes you nervous.

Exercise

Randy, a single, highly sensitive man in his late twenties, recently moved to the Bay Area and began working at a company where the major social activity was a weekly softball game. Although he had terrible memories of the pressure he experienced having to play group sports in school, he thought that he should join in the group activity since he didn't have many friends in the area.

However, when he went to play in the softball game he was the only player who didn't get a hit, and he made some errors, dropping the ball. After the game, he felt humiliated, angry, and sad. After that traumatic experience, he discovered a hiking club that met near his house on weekends. He began going on group hikes instead of playing softball and had a wonderful time meeting new friends by participating in a peaceful activity.

No Strain, Much to Gain

As HSPs, it's imperative to forego the popular Type A, competitive activities in favor of exercises that create inner peace. Additionally, in order to avoid injury, it's important to exercise at a pace that is comfortable for you. You should exercise at about 50 percent of your capacity and you should be able to carry on a conversation breathing through your nose. In 1996 the Surgeon General recommended that people engage in thirty minutes of moderate intensity physical activity on most, if not all, days. These activities can be broken up into several shorter sessions that add up to thirty minutes over the day (Jacobs 1998).

When I used to play basketball almost daily, I couldn't understand why I always felt tired. I didn't realize at the time that, as a sensitive man, I couldn't always keep up with some on the other athletes. However, when I reduced my intense aerobic activity to two or three times a week, I felt more energetic. While non-HSPs can sometimes engage in intense daily exercise, most HSPs have to carefully monitor the amount and degree of their physical activity. As long as you are slightly increasing your heart rate during a brisk twenty- to thirty-minute period of activity, you will be deriving many physical benefits without risking deleterious emotional or physical side effects.

Our competitive sports culture is anathema for many HSPs and can be especially challenging for males. Boys who are not athletic feel undervalued and suffer socially (Kindlon 1999). Many boys and girls are ostracized or teased if they are not adept in team sports at school. Playing group sports under pressure can create performance anxiety and can be overwhelming for the HSP, possibly creating poor self-esteem. More than 90 percent of the HSPs I surveyed reported that they prefer to participate in individual exercise rather than team sports. While some HSPs may be naturally athletic and, with practice, can cope with the pressure of team sports, individual and noncompetitive exercise is generally more in tune with the HSP temperament.

Steve, an HSP in his mid forties, reported that he used to feel overwhelmed by group pressure when he was forced to play team sports in school. He dreaded having to play baseball during gym classes when all eyes focused on him trying to catch a ball in right field. Due to the humiliation associated with sports, Steve avoided physical activity as a boy. However, as an adult Steve found that he actually enjoyed some individual and group sports. He realized that as long as he was not in a pressure situation while playing a game, he was able to perform well. When he played tennis with a supportive friend he excelled in the sport. However, whenever he played doubles with two strangers he would frequently become overwhelmed by the pressure and usually played poorly.

Peer pressure and trying to fit into a competitive sports culture can also be detrimental to your physical health. Steve related how he was working out at a health club several years ago with some friends and found himself trying to fit into a "non-HSP macho competition" to see who could lift the most weight, resulting in a torn tendon in his shoulder

You don't need to shun all group activities, but use discrimination about when to participate in an activity and when to refrain from an exercise that could be harmful. Alice, an HSP woman in her thirties, told me that she detests swimming in cold water unless it's a really hot day since she is very sensitive to the cold. One day in March she and a group of her friends went to a lake, and since the day was warm, everyone decided to take a dip in the icy water. Alice initially didn't want to go in, but after observing others swimming and slowly testing the water, she finally decided to take a dip. She said that it wasn't initially a pleasant thought to submerge her sensitive body in the freezing water, but since it was only for a few seconds she went ahead and took the plunge. She reported that it actually felt refreshing, and she was glad that she pushed herself to go beyond her normal limits in that situation.

Fun and Games for the HSP

Generally, it's best for HSPs to engage in noncompetitive sports such as walking, riding a bike, or yoga. There are also many new cooperative games that groups of people can play, such as keeping a large ball in the air. One of my most memorable experiences on the basketball court was when a friend and I pretended we were playing against an imaginary team, enjoying the camaraderie of our cooperative fantasy game.

One of the easiest and least expensive exercises for healing your body and mind is to take a silent walk in nature every day. While hiking amongst natural beauty, you may want to also practice a walking meditation. As I mentioned in chapter 3, it's important to stay focused in the present moment when we are walking in nature.

However, if you enjoy competing in sports, it's probably best to play with just one other supportive person to reduce excessive stimulation. Alice, who pushed herself to take a dip in cold water, is wary of putting herself in dangerous situations. However, she said that once she foolishly went skiing for the first time with a competitive friend who was supposed to teach her how to ski. Instead of teaching Alice on a beginner's slope, her non-HSP "friend" immediately took her to the top of a high ski slope. The non-HSP friend decided to ski down the hill rather than teaching Alice the fundamentals of skiing, leaving her alone in the cold snow not knowing what to do. Alice felt so humiliated that she took off the skis and walked down the slope. She never went skiing again.

If you or your HSP child wants to play team sports, choose a sport that is inherently less violent such as soccer or volleyball rather than American football or rugby. However, any player or coach with an insensitive attitude to win at all costs could turn any game into an HSP hell. Unfortunately, we are still living in a culture where "winning isn't everything—it's the only thing." Actually, any sport can be enjoyable if the consciousness of the participants is supportive and caring.

A method to exercise the body while reducing tension is hatha yoga, which originated in India but has become very popular in the West in recent years. Yoga postures consist of a series of stretching poses that tone the body while releasing stress. When you perform hatha yoga, not only are you exercising your body, but you are calming both your mind and nervous system. Proper yoga instructors will advice you to perform gentle movements and never to push yourself into a pose. Tai chi is another calming exercise, one that originated in China and is becoming very popular in the West. Tai chi consists of slow and harmonious martial-arts movements, which help promote a feeling of inner-peace for the participant.

In one of my HSP classes a student brought up a theory that if we do intense exercise we will be able to transcend the body and not be as sensitive to stimulation. However, for most HSPs, strong exercise creates overstimulation not inner-peace. Another student mentioned that she needed to feel more grounded in her body and found karate lessons helpful. I would say that gentle exercises such as hatha yoga would probably be more beneficial for centering yourself than taking a class in kick boxing or karate sparring. Every highly sensitive person is unique, so explore the type of exercise that works best for you.

Creating an Exercise Schedule

During exercise the body releases endorphins, which actually reduce stress. A hundred years ago, when people did a lot of manual labor and walked more, endorphins were being released throughout the day, resulting in less stress. The endorphins that are released account for the runner's high and the blissful feeling people experience after exercise. Besides reducing stress, regular aerobic exercise also reduces blood pressure and cholesterol, strengthens your heart, and helps you lose weight.

While exercising is helpful in losing weight, remember that during a thirty-minute jog you can only burn up the equivalent of a cup of frozen yogurt containing three hundred calories. When I was in my twenties, I played basketball almost every day for at least an hour. However, I couldn't understand why I kept gaining weight. I kept rationalizing that since I did heavy aerobic exercise almost every day it was okay to eat a lot of cookies or ice cream most nights. Twenty-five pounds later I had to drop my "it's fine to eat whatever you want if you exercise" theory.

It's generally not good to exercise after 7 P.M. since it takes about three hours for the body to cool down. I had a student in my stress-reduction class who told me that he had to exercise in the evening because he would be too exhausted throughout the day if he exercised earlier. Even though he mentioned that he was sensitive to stimuli, he was a very competitive man. When I inquired as to what type of exercise he did, he responded, "I go to the health club, turn the treadmill up to it's highest level, and run full blast for thirty minutes. Then I get on the Stairmaster and push as hard as I can for another half hour. Finally I work out with heavy weights for a half hour." I told him that I was getting tired just listening to his workout routine.

When we explored the issue of why he chose to exercise so intensely, he told me that he grew up with two tough older brothers who would always humiliate him and beat him in sports. He finally realized that he was overcompensating for having been in a physically weak position as a child. Once you investigate and understand the reasons for any addictive, out-of-balance behavior, it's easier to release the negative pattern.

If it's difficult for you to get off the couch, exercise with a friend, relative, or coworker in order to create a support system. Studies have found that if you exercise with a family member, your relationship will improve, since you're experiencing the release of endorphins together, creating a positive mutual experience (Bhat 1995). Create a regular exercise schedule with a buddy. Choose an exercise that you really enjoy and if you just plain hate to exercise, put your favorite tape in a headset and read an interesting book or magazine while on a stationary bike, treadmill, or Stairmaster machine. If you exercise at a health club, it's important to choose one that has a calming ambiance. An hour in a facility with loud, jarring music, bright fluorescent lights, and a crowd of noisy people could actually create more tension for the sensitive person. It's best to work out near your office or home so driving a long distance won't be a deterrent. You may want to consider buying equipment to use at home where you could watch an inspiring television show or a video while exercising. However, try to exercise outside in a natural environment as much as possible to reduce stimulation. Always consult your physician before you begin an exercise program.

Supplements, Vitamins, and Herbs

Given the HSPs proclivity to absorb stress that can create physical and emotional problems, it makes sense for us to use the effective supplements, vitamins, and herbal treatments that are available to help maintain our energy level, stay calm, and modify any adverse physiological reactions from stress. Research by Drs. Shamberger and Lonsdale found that patients who experienced fatigue, mood swings, and insomnia had fewer symptoms after six to twelve weeks of taking supplementary nutrients (Goldberg 1993). In my research, I found that most HSPs take supplements or herbs on a daily basis. As a matter of fact, an estimated 46 percent of adult Americans take nutritional supplements daily (Goldberg 1993). Some HSPs have told me that they are interested in taking supplements but feel overwhelmed and confused, not knowing which to take. The variety and number of choices available can be mind boggling, as the supplement business has become a billion dollar industry. Ten years ago you would rarely find herbs in your local pharmacy or supermarket, but now herbs and supplements can be found in most retail stores. No wonder so many people are confused!

In addition to the sheer number available, it can be hard to know where to turn for reliable information on supplements and herbs. Unfortunately, a situation has developed where millions of people are buying supplements and herbs, yet the American FDA (Federal Drug Administration) does not regulate the industry, and most medical doctors have not received any training in the use of supplements and herbs. In a recent study, 83 percent of physicians admitted that they had no formal training on drug and nutrient interactions (Whitaker 2004). To make matters more confusing for the consumer, some unscrupulous manufacturers trying to make a fast buck will be inconsistent in what they're actually offering to the public. Studies have shown that there are different amounts and qualities of herbs and supplements from various companies promoting the identical products (Whitaker 2004).

While generally herbs and supplements are safe, you always have to be careful about side effects. If you are already taking allopathic medicine (conventional medicines prescribed by your doctor or bought over the counter), you need to be especially aware of the effects that vitamins and herbs may have on your body. For example, some herbs and vitamin E can be dangerous to take with the medication coumadin, a blood thinner.

I strongly recommend that you consult with your physician before taking any herbs or supplements. However, as I mentioned, many medical doctors have limited knowledge about supplements and herbs. If your doctor is not familiar with a supplement, I recommend that you meet with a holistic medical doctor (see chapter 10). Interestingly, in many European countries doctors learn about herbs in medical school and routinely prescribe herbal formulas to their patients. I feel that it's just a question of time before American doctors learn about and prescribe supplements and herbs. Unfortunately, this quantum shift may not happen overnight due to the pharmaceutical industry's influence on the medical profession. However, I was recently surprised to find out that some American orthopedic physicians are now prescribing the supplement glucosamine for patients with joint problems.

There are many reputable medical doctors and medical researchers who have written books and articles describing the safe use of supplements and herbs for the public. There are also many holistic healers such as homeopaths, naturopaths, ayurvedic practitioners, herbalists, and acupuncturists who are knowledgeable in prescribing supplements and herbs. However, it's important to make sure that your practitioner is really well informed on all of the side effects. Chapter 10 explains more about these specialists and provides guidance in finding one for yourself.

You may find that you're more comfortable with a holistic health care practitioner because many of them are highly sensitive, while most medical doctors are not. It's important for you to let your doctor know that you are a highly sensitive person. Tell your doctor that since you tend to feel things more deeply, your body could react to medication and pain more intensely than most people. This is important information for your doctor to know about you.

I feel that it's important to utilize the excellent advances we've made in modern Western medicine in combination with ancient healing herbs from indigenous cultures, and modern supplements and vitamins. It would be beneficial for you to get an annual physical exam including all the necessary blood tests, which gives you excellent information about the state of your health. This information will help you in determining what supplements will serve you best, so that you will have a good understanding of which supplements to take. If you do not have outpatient health insurance, you may want to talk to the billing department at your local hospitals to determine the costs of laboratory tests. By shopping around, you may find that some hospitals give up to 75 percent off when you pay in advance for lab testing.

It's important to check prices of herbs and supplements before purchasing them. There are many discount health food stores. However, don't just buy a product because it's cheap since it's important to obtain the highest quality supplement from a reputable manufacturer. You may want to talk with the buyer who orders vitamins and herbs at your local health food store to determine which brand has a good reputation. Ask the clerk how long they have been working with herbs and vitamins. Unfortunately, some health food stores hire people with little or no experience, so make sure the person you talk to is well informed.

Always ask the salesperson when the herb or supplement was manufactured, since the expiration date may not be accurate. For example, flax seed oil should be used within six months or sooner of the date of manufacture, yet sometimes the expiration date will be in one or two years. When taking herbs, unless you can be sure that the capsules (or loose herbs in a jar) are fresh, it is better to buy a tincture (liquid preserved in an alcohol or non-alcohol base). After six months some dry herbs begin to lose their potency and in one year many herbs are not very effective at all. A tincture lasts for up to five years.

How to Find the Right Supplements and Herbs

There are some excellent sources available to obtain information on herbs and supplements. Julian Whitaker, M.D. (www.drwhitaker. com), the author of many articles and books on alternative healing, is the director of a wellness institute. Another excellent source is Andrew Weil, M.D. (www.drweil.com), who is perhaps the most well-known proponent of alternative medicine. In his books *Natural Health Natural Medicine* (1990) and *Spontaneous Healing* (1995), he recommends specific Western, Chinese, and Ayurvedic herbs. In Dr. Deepak Chopra's book *Grow Younger Live Longer* (2001), he offers important information on the proper use of supplements and herbs.

Jean Carper (www.stopagingnow.com) is an internationally known medical writer whose articles regularly appear in the magazine *USA Weekend*, found in many Sunday newspapers. Her informative book, *Stop Aging Now* (1995), contains the latest medical research on the benefits of supplements and herbs. She lists the proper dosage, the type of supplement to buy, and any potential adverse reactions. Some of the supplements she describes are vitamins B_{12}, C, and E, chromium, zinc, calcium, magnesium, selenium, and coenzyme Q-10.

There are many herbs and supplements you can take to reduce anxiety and tension. However, it's generally not a good idea to take herbal preparations for stress reduction daily since your body may become habituated to the herb and could need larger dosages for the herb to be effective. Herbs for anxiety relief should be taken on an "as needed" basis.

Some commonly used herbs to reduce anxiety are valerian, passionflower, hops, and chamomile. Many HSPs have had good results buying a formula with a combination of healing herbs, which creates a synergistic effect. While valerian is the most sedating herb, some people actually have reported the opposite reaction after taking valerian, finding it stimulating. Everyone's system reacts differently to each herb as well as to the dosage. Ask your doctor or health care practitioner what dosage you should take. Since HSPs are more sensitive to the effects of herbs, you should begin with a small dose and slowly increase the amount you take under your health care provider's advice. Experiment with different herbs to see which one works best for your constitution. Finally, there is a marvelous flower essence tincture called "Rescue Remedy" that helps create calmness during stressful situations.

Insomnia may occur when you travel or are under stress. You can take some calming herbs an hour before sleep. You may also want to try taking melatonin, which is the actual hormone that our brain releases when we go to sleep. You can take a time-released brand of melatonin an hour before bedtime to help you fall asleep or for jet lag. If you're traveling by plane through more than two or three time zones, you may experience jet lag, making it difficult for you to fall asleep even if you're extremely tired. A new homeopathic remedy called "No Jet Lag" can be helpful in reducing jet lag. There is more information about herbs and supplements for relaxation in the following chapter on better sleep.

If digestive problems occur due to stress you may want to take some aloe juice, gentian, or bitters. Chamomile and ginger tea can also soothe an upset stomach. A cup of chamomile tea is a great natural stress reducer. As I mentioned in chapter 3, packaged herb teabags may not be so potent. It's more effective to buy fresh chamomile or other calming herbs in capsules, open them up and put one tablespoon in a cup, add hot water, cover with a lid or small plate for at least five minutes, strain, and drink. Most Chinese herbs are prepared by boiling water containing the herbs down to 1 cup, then straining it.

A great deal of the information in this book is based on the principles of an ancient healing system from India called Ayurveda. Ayurveda can achieve similar effects as conventional medicines, but often with much less risk. For instance, the Ayurvedic herb guggul lowers cholesterol in a manner similar to pharmaceutical drugs but with less risk according to Dr. Andrew Weil. The herb triphala is the best bowel regulator Dr. Weil has ever found (1995). There are also herbs that calm the nervous system such as jatamamsi and ashwaghanda (Frawley 1989). Ayurvedic calming herbs in a sesame-oil base for external application are a potent relaxant that you may want to use when you're under stress (www.oilbath.com).

Although you may end up spending fifty dollars a month or more on supplements and herbs, this preventative measure is a fraction of what you could be spending on allopathic medicine if you don't maintain a healthy body and a tranquil mind. An ounce of prevention is worth a pound of cure!

A Healthy Diet to Reduce Stress

- Increase your intake of organic veggies, fruits, whole grains, low-fat protein, omega 3 oil (from salmon, flax seed oil, or fish oil), and herbal teas.

- Reduce your consumption of sugar, preservatives, salt, caffeine, high-glycemic foods, and processed foods.

- Eat all the lightly cooked, organic veggies or raw salad you want for lunch and dinner.

- When eating fattening meals, eat only half an average portion of the dish. Try to eat the heavy foods with awareness, very slowly, savoring each morsel.

- Between meals eat some fruit, veggies, nuts, seeds, or low-fat yogurt. Try to have healthy snacks available at home, at work, or when you go out.

- Especially when it's cold outside, it's calming and nurturing for the HSP's nervous system to eat heavy, warm, moist dishes such as hearty soups and casseroles.

- Buy a book that contains delicious, healthy recipes, and enlist the support of family and friends to follow your new diet.

An Exercise Program for the HSP

- Exercise with a buddy to create a support system. Exercise close to your home or workplace.

- Consider buying an exercise machine and place it in an area where you'll be likely to use it.

- Choose an exercise that you really enjoy. Try to do gentle exercises like walking, yoga, or tai chi, and avoid tense environments like overstimulating health clubs or very competitive team sports.

- Pace your exercise level to reinforce success. Don't feel exhausted or strained at the end of the session. Work out at 50 percent of your maximum capacity.

- Remember that regular aerobic exercise helps prevent heart disease, lowers blood pressure, helps you control weight, increases your energy and joy, and reduces stress and depression.

- It's best not to work out after 7 P.M. since it may create insomnia.

- If exercising is boring to you, listen to interesting tapes or CDs on a headset, watch an inspiring television show or video, or read a book or magazine while on an exercise machine.

- Try to exercise twenty to thirty minutes daily (taking a walk in nature is excellent for the HSP).

- Consult a physician before beginning an exercise program.

Taking Supplements and Herbs

- Utilize modern medical laboratory testing to help determine which supplements and herbs are best for you to take.

- Read books and visit Web sites of reputable holistic doctors to determine the best supplemental and herbal program for you.

- Meet with your health care provider to determine the dosage, brand, and possible adverse reactions of herbs and supplements.

- Make sure herbs are fresh or buy tinctures, which are potent for up to five years.

- It's best not to take high dosages of herbal preparations for anxiety and insomnia every day.

- Remember, an ounce of prevention is worth a pound of cure.

- Consult with your physician before taking herbs and supplements.

Sleepless No More: A Program for Better Sleep

$\mathcal{I}$n this chapter you will learn about the relationship between overstimulation and sleep. I'll be introducing numerous relaxation techniques to reduce overstimulation that will help the HSP with or without sleep challenges.

Overstimulation and Sleep Problems

In my research I found that many HSPs have occasional to frequent problems falling or staying asleep. When you become overaroused, it is more difficult for you to fall asleep. According to Elaine Aron, "Overstimulation is often the cause of sleeplessness in infants" (2002). It is also extremely difficult for most highly sensitive people to fall asleep with jarring background noise.

A few years ago a Harris poll indicated that 50 percent of adults have trouble sleeping and 15 percent of the population have chronic insomnia (Jacobs 1998). The insomniac usually has an easily aroused central nervous system and consequently faster brain-wave activity. Therefore, due to hyper-sensitivity to noise and difficulty relaxing after experiencing stimulation, the highly sensitive person often experiences challenges in being able to get a good night's sleep.

My Twenty-Year Bout with Insomnia

I remember clearly that I began having trouble falling asleep when I was in fifth grade. Not only was I extremely sensitive to problems I was having at school, which worried me at night, but I couldn't fall asleep if my dad was watching television in the next room or if I heard my parents talking. As an HSP it's been virtually impossible for me to tune out extraneous noise. I would also frequently wake up during the night and have difficulty falling back to sleep. The lack of sleep created a vicious cycle, with me worrying at night that I would be too tired the next day to function, which would then make me feel more anxious and over-aroused.

By the time I was in seventh grade I was given a tranquilizer in order to fall asleep. Throughout junior and senior high school I would usually have to take sleeping pills three nights a week as I became psychologically and physiologically addicted to the medication. I had to keep increasing the dosage in order to fall asleep and consequently had trouble functioning in the daytime due to grogginess. This insomniac pattern continued throughout my twenties. During sleepless nights I frequently experienced severe anxiety and near panic as I tossed and turned for hours in bed.

When I was thirty years old, I began studying for my Ph.D. in psychology and completed a great deal of research in the field of stress management and insomnia. During this time period I made important changes in my lifestyle. I began reducing my overstimulating Type A behavior, maintained an exercise schedule that was appropriate for my constitution, changed my diet, began implementing daily meditation and relaxation techniques, and developed a new, positive attitude toward sleep.

Through many years of research and experimentation, I created a successful sleep program and can happily report that I no longer suffer from insomnia. I usually fall asleep within a few minutes of turning off the light and I only experience some difficulty falling asleep a couple of times a year, either when I'm traveling or dealing with an extraordinarily stressful situation.

How did I end my twenty-year insomniac nightmare of sleeping pills, anxiety, and fear? What is the method that has healed insomnia in so many of my students who have taken my classes? Some students have said my voice is so boring that it puts them right to sleep. I tell my students that if they fail the insomnia course, it's nothing to lose sleep over. Seriously, I've found that keeping my sense of humor has been an important ingredient in helping me overcome my own insomnia. When HSPs become too serious about their sensitivity and insomnia, sleep challenges are magnified. But, aside from a few laughs, this chapter will bring you all the wisdom I gained in my twenty year struggle.

Our Culture Encourages Sleep Problems

If your insomnia is not due to physiological causes, your finely tuned central nervous system is probably the major component that inhibits a restful sleep. The insomnia is likely just a symptom of the HSP trying to fit their round peg of a central nervous system into the square hole of an overstimulating society. As we look deeper into the causes of the HSP's sleeplessness, you'll understand the important relationship between trying to conform to the mores of an overwhelming world and insomnia.

A hundred years ago people rarely suffered from insomnia (Zeff 1999). There was no road rage, overstimulating television, or computers. Our great grandparents didn't watch the war of the week brought into their homes in living, gory color through the medium of television.

In the beginning of the twentieth century, more people lived in small towns or rural areas and were attuned to the peace and harmony in nature. There is something to the old adage of "early to bed, early to rise," which was commonplace before the advent of electricity. Compare living in a serene, natural environment 100 years ago to driving in rush hour in any of our large urban cities and you can understand why insomnia has become endemic to modern life. How can you easily fall asleep if you're acclimatized to a stressful environment where your muscles are chronically tense and your mind is racing with stimulating thoughts?

When you live in a chronic state of tension, stress hormones activate your central nervous system. You become habituated to increased muscles tension, heart rate, and blood pressure as well as heightened sensory acuity. All these factors promote insomnia. Recent research has shown that stress hormones raised during the day also remain elevated at night while you sleep (Jacobs 1998).

The first step in making changes to reduce insomnia is to evaluate your life goals. The HSP needs to make a concerted effort to create a lifestyle that minimizes overstimulation. By spending time each day in self-reflection, pondering how to obtain the goal of inner-peace, you will be able to clearly identify where you can make positive changes in your life and understand what motivates you to stay stuck in a stressful work or home situation. But try to remember that in our overstimulating world, we have become habituated to instant gratification. You may have experienced insomnia for some time, so you will need patience as you slowly reduce your sleep problems. Try not to get discouraged if you still have trouble sleeping while implementing some of the suggestions in this chapter. Little by little, your sleep will definitely improve.

Different Stages of Sleep

There are five stages of sleep: two levels of light sleep, two levels of deep sleep, and dream sleep. Stage one is a transition between wakefulness and sleep. What are called "theta" brain wave patterns emerge during light sleep, which is similar to a deep state of relaxation. Stage one lasts only a few minutes. Stage two, light sleep, is the first real stage of sleep. People spend half the night in stage two light sleep (Jacobs 1998).

Deep sleep (stages three and four) create what are known as "delta" brain wave patterns. The body is at its deepest rest, with blood pressure and heart rate at their lowest levels. The deep sleep stage is the most important part of sleep. Deep sleep occurs more frequently during the beginning of the night and while in deep sleep the immune system turns on. However, stress hormones (such as epinephrine), secreted from overstimulation during the day can continue to be released in the body during sleep. When you don't reach stages three and four during the night, there is a tendency for your immune system to be compromised (Jacobs 1998).

REM (rapid eye movement) or the dream state is a lighter stage of sleep resembling wakefulness. There are approximately four ninety-minute cycles of sleep each night in which we experience all four stages and REM sleep. During the first part of the night deep sleep cycles are longer and REM sleep is minimal, but as the night progresses stages three and four lessen while the REM sleep pattern increases.

Research indicates that five and a half hours of core, deep sleep is enough to function adequately throughout the day, and less than five hours can still be sufficient if a nap is taken the next day (Jacobs 1998). After five and a half hours of core sleep, 100 percent of deep sleep and 50 percent of REM sleep is completed. People frequently wake up when going from REM to light sleep. Even if you wake up at 4 A.M., if you got to sleep at 10:30 P.M. you've completed all your important deep sleep, so there is no need to worry about falling back to sleep. When depressed patients have been deprived of excessive dream sleep, they actually improved, since too much dreaming is emotionally and physically fatiguing. Studies show it's better for depressed patients to get up early to avoid excessive dream sleep (Jacobs 1998).

With five to six hours of sleep, your performance won't drop off, but you may feel a little tired during the day. Some people are more creative at night. Thomas Edison worked at night and slept only a few hours each morning and afternoon. You may discover you actually need less sleep than you think.

When you meditate or relax deeply, your body receives the rest that is equivalent to light sleep. If you experience difficulty falling asleep but spend that time either meditating or performing deep relaxation, you will feel rested the following day. This is the reason why many meditators do not need much sleep. Also, during meditation there is reduced secretion of stress hormones (Zeff 1999). There is also a reduction in heart and breathing rates, as well as relaxation of the muscles.

Research performed at sleep clinics has indicated that many people who claimed that they didn't sleep a wink at night actually slept for hours (Jacobs 1998). The subjects thought that they were awake during their light sleep stage. In addition, when someone is in a stressed state, time seems to slow down, so the time you're lying awake during the night can feel longer. In a study at the Stanford University Sleep Clinic, 122 insomniacs overestimated the time it took them to fall asleep by thirty minutes and underestimated total sleep time by one hour (Jacobs 1998).

Everyone requires a different amount of sleep. I have a friend who has slept for only five hours a night throughout her life, and she functions well on that amount of sleep. Other people require nine hours of sleep to feel well rested. The amount of sleep your constitution requires changes throughout your life. Frequently, if you believe that you've had enough sleep, you won't be tired the next day. I remember one busy day I was feeling energetic after having slept only five hours the previous night. As soon as I calculated the small amount of sleep that I'd had, I suddenly became exhausted and wanted to lie down.

Try going to bed and getting up at the same time each day. If you sleep late on Sunday morning, you may not be sleepy at bedtime, setting yourself up for "beginning of the week insomnia syndrome." It's tempting to sleep late on or take long naps during the day, but it could compromise your sleep at night. Try not to nap for more than thirty minutes. However, taking a short nap instead of coffee will improve productivity and mood for the rest of the day.

Physiological Causes for Sleep Problems

It's important to rule out any medical issues that may be causing insomnia. If you've been told that you seem to gasp for air during the night, snore loudly, and wake up feeling tired even after "sleeping " a long time, you may have sleep apnea (Zeff 1999). People with sleep apnea literally wake up hundreds of times during the night due to breathing that is obstructed, but they are not aware that they've awoken. There are some relatively simple procedures that can be implemented to help people who are suffering from sleep apnea.

Another medical condition that can cause sleep difficulties is restless leg syndrome (Zeff 1999). It can cause unpleasant sensations in the leg while lying down or involuntary twitching of the leg. *Bruxism* or tooth grinding can also interfere with your sleep. If you suspect that a medical condition is interfering with your sleep, consult with your doctor, who can refer you to a sleep clinic. There are sleep clinics located in every major metropolitan area that can evaluate your sleep problem.

Another important consideration is to determine if any medication that you're taking could be interfering with your sleep, either causing insomnia at night by acting as a stimulant or grogginess during the day, creating sedation. Over-the-counter medication can also disturb sleep. Some analgesics contain caffeine and some nasal decongestants and asthma medications have a stimulating effect (Jacobs 1998). Check with your physician to find out the possible side effects of any medication or combination of medications that you're currently taking. You may also want to consult with your pharmacist. I recommend that older people consider consulting with a gerontologist, who is knowledgeable regarding the effects of medications for seniors. You may also want to research the side effects of medication at your local library or on the Internet.

Sleeping Pills and Herbal Preparations

Scientific studies have shown that a behavioral treatment for insomnia is more effective than a pharmacological approach. According to the National Institute of Health and the *New England Journal of Medicine*, insomnia should be treated by behavioral, nondrug approaches (Jacobs 1998). Sleeping pills become increasingly ineffective with regular use and can cause many side effects. In the 1970s, sleeping pills were the most widely prescribed medication in the world. They still account for $400 million dollars in annual sales. The most frequently prescribed sleeping pills are called benzodiazepines, which are safer than the older sleeping pills, barbiturates. The benzodiazepines with a short half-life (the time it takes the body to break down and eliminate them) will usually not cause drowsiness the next day. Ambien's half-life is only 1.5 to 4.5 hours, while Valium takes two to five days to leave the body (Jacobs 1998).

According to Andrew Weil, M.D., if you are experiencing a major trauma, it may be appropriate to take a sedative drug for a few nights (1995). However, taking them every night is not wise. All sedatives present problems. They depress the function of the central nervous system, can eventually create a psychological and physiological addiction, suppress REM (dream activity), produce grogginess during the day, and may require larger dosages due to developing tolerance.

However, if you are regularly taking sleeping medication, don't worry. As you slowly integrate the holistic approaches to sleep described in this chapter your sleep will improve. Patients should gradually taper off sleeping medication only under the supervision of their doctor. You may want to begin a program whereby one night a week (choose the easiest night to fall asleep) you take half the normal dosage. Then slowly decrease the dosage on other nights. You will become more confident as you slowly learn to sleep without medication.

Many people have reported good results when they occasionally take an herbal formula containing a mixture of herbs such as valerian root, passion flower, or skullcap. Others have reported good results by taking the minerals calcium and magnesium, which produce a calming effect on the nervous system. However, if you take herbs every night, your body can develop a tolerance just as it does with sleeping pills, and you may need to keep increasing the dosage. Please see chapter 4 on supplements and herbs for more information.

Preparing for Sleep

It's important to prepare yourself for sleeping. After all it doesn't make much sense to go from your wakeful, daytime life right into bed and expect to drift into restful sleep. But that's what many of us do. Following are some strategies to help you make the transition from alert and awake to peaceful slumber.

Consciously Relax

Meditating, doing progressive relaxation (visualizing your muscles relaxing), or listening to a relaxation tape for approximately twenty minutes before bedtime will help reduce sleep problems by quieting the mind and relaxing the body. In addition, meditation and deep relaxation breaks throughout the day may reduce stress hormones from being secreted at night, promoting better sleep. While it's optimal to do deep relaxation or meditation for at least twenty minutes twice a day, even meditating for a few minutes every hour will help lessen your stress level. You may want to encourage your family members to meditate with you in the evening. Meditation can also reduce nocturnal familial conflicts. A family that meditates together will not need to mediate together.

Early to Bed

The optimal time to go to bed for most HSPs is by 10 P.M. According to Deepak Chopra, it's easier to fall asleep before 10 P.M. due to the natural biorhythms of the day (1994). Have you ever found yourself getting sleepy early in the evening, but then feeling wide-awake at midnight? Just like flowers that close their petals at dusk and non-nocturnal animals that go to sleep a little after the sun sets, it's more natural for most people to fall asleep by 10 P.M.(Lad 1984). If you're currently going to bed near midnight or later, try going to bed fifteen minutes earlier each week and in a few months your bedtime will be closer to 10 P.M. Of course, some schedules make going to bed early difficult, so just do the best you can. You may want to experiment by going to bed earlier for a week and notice if you can fall asleep more easily.

No Time No Problem

One of the most important rules to follow to reduce sleep problems is never ever look at a clock or watch after 8 P.M. (Zeff 1999). Many of my students have had amazing success in stopping their insomniac pattern by just following this simple rule. The mind needs a negative hook to perpetuate sleep problems, and one of the best cues to create a sleep disorder is to look at the clock and worry about not getting enough sleep. How can you possibly fall asleep if you're overstimulating your mind worrying about what time it is? You may want to put your clocks in obscure places so you're not always looking at them. It may also help release your time-urgent behavior to not wear a watch or frequently look at the clock during the day.

Alan, a married HSP in his thirties, suffered from insomnia that was aggravated by his time-urgent behavior. Alan told me that his entire body would shake with frustration whenever he drove home on the congested freeways during rush hour. He was on a downward spiral, perceiving both time and other drivers on the road as his enemy. I recommended that Alan stop wearing his watch and not look at the clock at home or in his car. I also suggested that he spend some time in the "timeless" beauty of nature. The following week he and his wife came into my class smiling, exuding a state of deep inner-peace. Not only did Alan relinquish his watch, but he also went to Yosemite National Park for a long weekend where he and his wife did not look at a clock for three days. He reported that he had never experienced such a profound state of peace and joy in his life! By not worrying about time and being in a calm environment, Alan's anxiety and insomnia was transformed into bliss.

Turning Off the Media

It's best not to watch stimulating television shows or movies at night. By watching the nightly news you'll be inviting the murderer of the day into your consciousness right before going to sleep, which is hardly a peaceful lullaby. It's important to use discrimination when watching television. Always remember to click the mute button during advertisements so that you won't have to subject your nervous system to increased levels of overarousal. Use that time instead to take a meditation break whereby you can buy some inner-peace, rather than exposing yourself to the myriad of sense desires that the commercials are trying to sell you.

I have an HSP friend who won't watch movies or television any-more since she found that most shows have at least some gratuitous vio-lence that gives her anxiety and nightmares. However, since everyone responds differently to media stimulation, it's important to create a bal-anced lifestyle that works for you. I had one student who claimed that the only way she could fall asleep at night was watching television. While the television evidently gave her some sense of comfort, this approach can be quite detrimental for most HSPs.

Partner Problems

If your partner is a restless sleeper or snores loudly, severely dis-turbing your sleep, you need to consider obtaining twin beds or even sleeping in separate rooms. If your partner is a non-HSP who falls asleep as soon as their head hits the pillow, you need to help them understand how important it is for you to create a quiet environment in order to get a good night's sleep. You may want to see a marriage counselor if you can't work out a compromise that works for both of you.

Turn off the Day

After 8 or 9 P.M turn the answering machine to the lowest volume, turn off your cell phone, television, and computer and just let go of the day. As mentioned in chapter 2 on techniques to reduce overstimulation, your evening routine for most nights should consist of calming activities like reading spiritually uplifting books, meditating, or writing. Do not engage in any intense discussions late at night. As discussed in chapter 3, you may want to massage yourself with medicated oils or take a bath with a few drops of essential oil of lavender in the evening.

If you find yourself ruminating on a specific problem, spend up to an hour, if necessary, writing down every possible solution to the dilemma. Afterwards, realize that if you spend anymore time thinking about the situation, it will not help you one iota in solving the problem. So just let it go. Finally, spend some time writing down everything that you're grateful for in your life (Zeff 1999). It will be easier for you to fall asleep saturated with cheerful thoughts gently flowing through your mind.

Transform Your Room into a Womb

To reduce stimulation your bedroom should be a quiet, dark, and safe space. Since HSPs startle easily, you need to feel secure in your room to lessen any anticipatory danger. If you see a strange car idling in front of your house, your central nervous system can become easily aroused. It may be beneficial to try to sleep in a room in the rear of the house to reduce stimulation from street disturbances. Whenever you check into a motel or hotel, always ask for a quiet room away from the street.

In *The Highly Sensitive Child*, Elaine Aron described how her infant son slept better when he was snuggled in a sleeping tent covered with blankets, with no light and little noise (Aron 2002). What she described was a safe womb-like environment that would also help the HSP adult sleep better.

One highly sensitive student told me that she didn't feel safe in her bedroom due to some recent burglaries in her neighborhood. Although she put in a burglar alarm and many safety devices, she still had trouble falling asleep. Given her sensitivity to possible danger, she was unable to relax enough to fall asleep. When she finally moved to a new home in a safer neighborhood, her insomnia virtually disappeared.

A sense of serenity is increased by soft, warm colors such as white, light blue, and light green. Pictures in the bedroom should be cheerful, such as nature scenes like Monet's *Water Lilies*. By the way, Monet created murals of water lilies from his magnificent flower garden at Giverny as a gift of tranquility to the war-torn French after World War I (Murray 1997). Plants and flowers in your room will also create a nurturing, serene environment.

It's easier to fall asleep when the body is not overheated. The expression "it's too hot to sleep" is based on the reality that when it's extremely hot, the body cannot cool down enough to fall asleep. Try to keep the temperature in your bedroom at around 66 degrees or less (Zeff 1999). If you get cold, you can always pile blankets on top of you. Taking a bath or soaking in a hot tub in the evening (which deeply relaxes the muscles) is permissible since the body temperature falls quickly after immersion in hot water.

If you are overheated you may want to apply coconut oil (which is the most cooling oil) to your body or drink limewater. There is a yogic breathing exercise called *sheetali pranayama* that cools down your entire body (Zeff 1999). It is performed by curling your tongue into a tube, while breathing deeply through your mouth into your abdomen. Try doing a few rounds of this breathing exercise to cool down your body.

Some of my HSP students have reported that when they feel cold, they have had trouble sleeping. They felt that the cold increased their feeling of fear and anxiety, and they consequently preferred warm weather. Sometimes cold climates can make you feel less nurtured, while warm weather can have a soothing effect on your nervous system. If you live in a cold climate, it's important to stay warm during the winter.

Creating a Quiet and Dark Room

Noise is one of the most difficult challenges for HSPs, one that can interfere with getting a good night's sleep. Have you ever experienced one of the following scenarios: You've just spent several hours reducing stimulation by taking a bath, meditating, or reading a spiritually uplifting book. You are getting so drowsy that you can barely reach over to turn off the light. Just as you have entered stage one of light sleep, the neighbor's dog starts ferociously barking, jolting your entire nervous system, startling you awake. Or perhaps your upstairs neighbors begin blasting their music as they stomp around above you just as you're trying to fall asleep. Besides talking to your neighbors, moving your room (or in desperate situations moving your home), what can you do to deal with noise pollution that prevents you from getting a good night's sleep?

A white noise machine strategically placed near your head helps drown out startling noises while the mind subconsciously focuses on the constant sound. The hum of a soothing fan, air conditioner, or air purifier also masks disturbing noises. Sound machines offer different sounds from nature, such as the flow of a river. However, I don't think an HSP would find listening to the rain channel with intermittent crashing thunder very soothing.

Another effective method to reduce noise is wearing earplugs. The wax earplugs have a noise reduction rate of twenty-two decibels while the foam earplugs usually have at least a twenty-nine-decibel reduction rate. Some people have not found foam earplugs effective due to the fact that they are sometimes difficult to fully seal in the ear. You need to follow the directions carefully to insert the earplugs correctly. Also, some people have ear canals that are not conducive for inserting the foam earplugs fully.

As I mentioned in chapter 3, earmuff-style headsets, which are used by construction workers are effective in reducing sound. They reduce sound by approximately twenty-two decibels and you can buy the headsets at hardware stores. While most people might find them difficult to sleep in, one student reported falling asleep on his back and then while asleep he instinctively removed them so he could turn over on his side.

An audiologist can fit you for a custom-made set of earplugs that reduce sound by twenty-nine decibels. The advantage of the specially made earplugs is that they fit easily into your ear canal. Sometimes the custom earplugs need to be remolded if they don't feel comfortable. If you really want to tune out loud noises completely, try wearing a headset over earplugs.

Light sensitivity may also interfere with your sleep. Sometimes just a small amount of light coming through the cracks of a dark bedroom door is enough to create stimulation and keep you awake. You can put a sweep on the bottom of your bedroom door and weather stripping material along the cracks. You may want to buy some heavy drapes that block out light from the street or a full moon.

It's best not to be exposed to bright light before going to sleep. The light can create wakefulness. However, it's important to expose yourself to sunlight or some bright indoor lighting upon arising in the morning (Zeff 1999). Light stops the production of melatonin, the hormone that helps us sleep, aiding us in feeling more awake in the morning.

You can also buy a comfortable eye mask. Some of them now come with a built in headset. If you can tolerate a nightlight, it would be less stimulating than turning on a bright lamp if you go to the bathroom during the night. Being exposed to a bright light could make it difficult to fall back asleep. However, make sure that you have an easily accessible reading lamp next to your bed so that when you feel drowsy you don't have to get out of bed to turn off the light. To avoid waking up during the night with back pain your bed should also be comfortable. One student told me that she woke up constantly during the night with an aching back. However, once she bought a firm mattress, she slept better and would wake up in the morning pain free.

How Exercise and Diet Affect Sleep

As we saw in the last chapter, regular exercise reduces anxiety since your body releases endorphins that actually reduce stress. If you've been sitting all day in front of a computer, you may be restless at night and want to move around when you should be physically tired and ready for sleep. A lack of physical exercise can also contribute to insomnia by inhibiting the daily rise and fall of body temperature (Jacobs 1998). Exercise raises body temperature, which is followed by a drop three hours later, promoting sleep. It's not good to exercise in the evening because the body needs those three hours to cool down. If you want to exercise in the early evening you can go for a slow walk or do some gentle yoga postures.

Lena, a single HSP in her twenties, had a passion for dancing. Unfortunately, her dance classes and performances most often took place late at night. She continually complained that when she wanted to fall asleep at midnight she would toss and turn for hours even though she was physically exhausted. How could she possibly fall asleep after being overstimulated, raising her body temperature, and trying to fall asleep at midnight (a more stimulating time)? Lena was in quite a dilemma since she refused to give up her regular dance schedule. Interestingly, many non-HSPs would still be able to fall asleep after participating in the same stimulating activity. Since she refused to give up dancing, I suggested that she could either explore the possibility of pursuing her hobby in the late afternoon or early evening. However, if she maintained her present routine, she would continue to have sleep problems. By the way, I don't think the song "I Could Have Danced All Night" was written by an HSP.

It's beneficial to finish eating a light dinner by 7 P.M., and it's better to eat spicy foods for lunch rather than for dinner. Since it takes two to three hours to digest a meal, late-night dinners could contribute to insomnia. Eating some complex carbohydrates such as a piece of sprouted bread or some rye crackers before bedtime can increase serotonin, a brain neurotransmitter that may induce sleep. However, eating most forms of protein can inhibit sleep by blocking the synthesis of serotonin (Jacobs 1998).

Eating foods that are heavy, warm, and moist may help promote sleep. This kind of diet is both nurturing and centering, especially in the winter. One HSP tried going on a raw food diet. She told me that as soon as she began the diet, she started having trouble sleeping. Once she returned to a diet of cooked foods, she reported that she felt calmer and slept better. I recommend eating more cooked vegetables in the winter and more salads in the summer.

Drinking some warm milk with nutmeg an hour before bedtime may help you sleep. Nutmeg has natural calming properties (Frawley 1989). Also, drinking a glass of herb tea (such as chamomile) in the evening can relax the nervous system. Minimizing the use of caffeine such as coffee, black tea, chocolate, and soft drinks will reduce stimulation and promote better sleep.

Two final activities that can interfere with sleep is smoking, which is a stimulant, and drinking alcohol. While having a glass of wine with dinner will generally not adversely affect you and may actually relax you, it's important to monitor the effects of your alcohol intake. While several drinks of alcohol may calm some sensitive people, it can also cause a lighter and more restless sleep.

Reframe Your Thoughts about Sleep

One of the most important rules of improving your sleep is to develop a positive attitude. Negative thoughts about sleep can create a self-fulfilling prophecy that increases insomnia. You need to reframe any negative thinking into positive thoughts about sleep. Frequently, your fearful thoughts about sleep problems are not even true.

During my twenty years of insomnia, I vividly remember lying awake at night in severe anxiety, worrying about not being able to fall asleep. I kept writing the script each night for insomnia by believing pessimistic thoughts. Unfortunately, during my sleep-deprived years I didn't understand that my negative thoughts created a stressful physiological reaction. How could I have possibly fallen asleep when my fearful thinking caused a rapid heart rate, higher blood pressure, tense muscles, and shallow breathing?

The following are examples of negative thoughts that create insomnia followed by new, positive thoughts that can help eliminate sleep problems.

✺ "I have to drive for several hours tomorrow, and I'll never be able to drive that far without sleep. I might fall asleep at the wheel and get into an accident. I know—I'll drink coffee to get me through. But then I'll get all nervous and won't be able to sleep tomorrow night."

"As long as I get my core sleep of about five and a half hours, I won't have any problem driving. I can always take a short nap if I'm sleepy, which will help me feel alert. I'm not going to try to fall asleep. I'm just going to meditate and relax my muscles as I breathe slowly and deeply. Meditation is equivalent to light sleep, so I'll be fine tomorrow."

✺ "Oh no, I must have been lying awake now for a long time! The light is out at my neighbor's house, and I know they stay up till after midnight. It's one of those nights that I know I'll never fall asleep. I'll never be able to function tomorrow at work."

"I still have plenty of time to fall asleep. I've gone with a lot less sleep for one night without any difficulty. I don't need eight hours of sleep to function. I'll repeat the mantra "peace." That always works to calm me down.

Then I think I'll just enjoy reading my book. That also
relaxes me. When I'm drowsy later on, I'll fall asleep."

Some people create sleep problems by negative self-talk related to
time, such as:

- ✄   "Oh my gosh, it's already midnight and I haven't gotten
  ready for bed. I have to hurry up and get to bed so I can
  have enough sleep tonight." (Hurry up to relax—I don't
  think so!)

- ✄   "Oh no it's 2 A.M. and I still can't fall asleep. Now it's
  3:30, and I have to get up in a few hours and I still
  haven't gotten any sleep. What am I going to do?"

- ✄   "I hope I can fall back to sleep. I wonder what time it is.
  Oh no, it's 2 A.M., which means I've only slept for three
  hours. If I can't fall back to sleep, I'm in real trouble."

You can easily release any negative self-talk about time. Since
you're now going to go to bed by 10 P.M. simply tell yourself that you
have many hours to relax in bed and you will still have plenty of time to
obtain your core sleep. As a matter of fact, your goal is not to fall asleep
right away, but just to spend some time enjoying relaxation before sleep
by meditating or reading. Since you are not looking at the clock, a positive affirmation is: "It's still early, so I have plenty of time to fall asleep."

If you wake up during the night simply tell yourself: "I think it's
almost dawn, and I've probably had my core sleep of five and a half
hours. So it doesn't matter if I fall back to sleep or not. I'll just enjoy
relaxing for awhile." If you awaken during the night, it may be helpful to
keep focusing on the dream you've just had rather than immediately
begin worrying about either your daily problems or not being able to fall
back to sleep.

Never lie in bed trying to figure out how many hours you will have
slept that night. On the rare night that you may find yourself tossing in
bed sleepless for a long time, it's better to get out of bed rather than lying
there "trying" to sleep. You can read in bed or meditate lying down for
approximately an hour. However, if you are not drowsy after some time,
you could associate your bed with wakefulness, which could trigger a

negative cue. At that point it's better to get up and read, meditate, or listen to a relaxing tape until you become sleepy.

A Tale of Two Indian Cities: An HSP on the Road

It was the best of times, and it was the worst of times in India. On my first trip to India I naively didn't take any precautions against sleep problems. Traveling inherently creates insomnia due to sensitivity to change, overstimulation, and jet lag. Since I hadn't experienced sleep problems in many years, I foolishly didn't bring any herbal or allopathic sleeping aids on my first trip to India.

When I arrived in Madras after more than thirty-five hours of traveling, I was totally overwhelmed from the jet lag and the overstimulation of arriving in a third world country. Every sense organ was literally thrown into a state of shock. In order to save money my friend and I chose to stay in a hotel that was listed in a guidebook as a moderately priced Indian-style hotel. Since it was late at night and our taxi had left the hotel, I decided to take the room sight unseen. As I trudged up the narrow, dimly lit corridor, I was horrified to learn that the room was facing the busiest street in Madras. A rather unusual Indian custom is that every driver keeps one hand glued to the horn. The cacophony of screeching noises sent shivers down my spine. Los Angeles is like a breath of fresh air compared to the pollution in some of the large cities in India.

Unfortunately, the air conditioner in the barren room didn't work, so the only way to survive in the 98 degree humid heat was by opening the caked and cracked dirty window. The stained, torn sheets and aroma of urine emanating from the bathroom hardly helped to relax my olfactory sense. This was definitely not a safe, quiet, cool, and calming environment. While my non-HSP friend slept like a baby during that infamous night, I unfortunately had to keep constantly waking her up seeking support for severe anxiety that was bordering on panic. I felt like I had died and entered HSP hell. It was literally the worst night of my life.

Let's fast-forward thirteen years later to my second trip to India. This time my friend and I chose to fly into a smaller town in India and avoid the noisy and polluted large cities. Immediately upon arriving in the country, we went to a quiet beach resort, which was a short ride from the airport. I decided to splurge and stayed at an expensive, comfortable hotel the first night. I inspected the room thoroughly and was ready to ask for a different sleeping chamber if it wasn't really quiet. The lovely room contained an excellent air conditioner and a view of the beach.

On this second trip I took both allopathic and herbal sleep remedies as well as calming oils, an earmuff-style headset, earplugs, a headset tape player, and a sleep mask. Since my nervous system was wired from jet lag and overstimulation due to the long journey, I immediately took a small dose of a mild allopathic sleeping pill at bedtime. The next thing I knew, light from the sun rising over the Arabian Sea was pouring into my room. Since I had also taken a homeopathic remedy on the plane to minimize jet lag, I awoke that first morning full of energy and joy, ready to explore the fascinating new world that I had just entered.

I didn't have to take any more allopathic medication for the duration of the trip, and even though it was noisy at times, the headset and earplugs masked any obtrusive sounds. By applying calming oils and occasionally taking some herbs in the evening, I slept easily during the month-long sojourn in India. I had a blissful experience during my second, well-prepared journey.

As my story shows, it's important for you to take good care of yourself when you travel, and remember not to feel guilty about needing special preparations. If you're going to be a houseguest, let the host know about your special needs before you leave home. It's better to make other sleeping arrangements than stay in an untenable situation. As illustrated in my first trip to India, your non-HSP partner and friends can usually fall asleep even under the most austere conditions. When you plan ahead, both you and your non-HSP relatives and friends will be glad you did. However, you don't need to plan in a hypochondriac manner, worrying about every possible scenario that could go wrong. If you are spending the night at your new lover's house, you don't need to be like a Woody Allen movie character and pack two suitcases full of medication. Just take the minimal necessities to feel comfortable.

You will likely experience jet lag more profoundly than non-HSPs. Many of my students have reported that taking the homeopathic remedy

"No Jet Lag" (sold in health food stores) has helped minimize jet lag. Some people have also reported good results from taking melatonin. If you are experiencing insomnia due to jet lag, it is one of those rare times when it's okay to take a small dosage of a mild sleeping pill. While flying to your destination, make sure to drink plenty of fluids and try to stay awake on the plane during the time zone of your new destination and sleep or meditate when it is nighttime there. Do not sleep during the day when you arrive in the new time zone. Make sure that you have plenty of time to just relax during your first few days in your new location. By following these simple procedures, your trip will be the best of times for you too!

Reducing Sleep Problems

- Review your lifestyle, seeing where you're able to reduce stress.

- Rule out any medical causes for insomnia like medication, sleep apnea, etc.

- Twenty minutes before bedtime meditate, do deep abdominal breathing, progressive relaxation, or listen to a relaxation tape.

- Try to go to bed before or near 10 P.M.

- Don't look at a clock after 8 or 9 P.M.

- It's best not to watch stimulating television shows at night or engage in intense discussions. Spend the evening reading uplifting books, writing, meditating, or engaging in calm discussions.

- Take a silent walk in nature during the day.

- Do aerobic exercise for thirty minutes at least three times a week. Don't exercise in the evening.

- Finish eating a light dinner by 7 P.M. and don't eat spicy foods for dinner. Eating some starchy foods such as sprouted bread before bedtime can increase your sedative neurotransmitters.

- One hour before bedtime you can drink a glass of a calming herb tea, such as chamomile, or some warm milk with nutmeg.

- Take a bath with a few drops of essential oil of lavender or apply soothing oils to your body or forehead before going to bed.

- You can occasionally take some mild herbs an hour before bedtime such as passion flower or hops.

- Make sure your bedroom is quiet, dark, and at a cool temperature. The room should be a safe and nurturing space.

- Stick to a regular routine by going to bed and getting up at the same time each day.

- Develop a positive attitude toward sleep. Reframe negative self-talk about sleep into positive statements.

- Traveling may create sleep challenges, so take the necessary sleep aids with you.

Sweet dreams!

6

Harmonious Relationships for the HSP

*I*n the previous chapters we discussed methods to reduce overstimulation in our daily life and how stimuli affects our sleep. We are now going to investigate how being a highly sensitivity person influences relationships and learn techniques to create positive relationships with all sentient beings.

Sensitivity and Relationships

As an HSP you may sometimes tend to overreact to other people's moods and behavior, often negatively. The 40 percent of highly sensitive people who have experienced a difficult childhood tend to interact with people from a place of fear (Aron 2001). In the book, *The Highly Sensitive Person in Love*, Elaine Aron succinctly describes the highly sensitive person in intimate relationships (2001). In her landmark research of over one thousand people, she found that HSPs experience a deeper intensity when they fall in love than non-HSPs. She pointed out that 70 percent of HSPs are introverted and shy and speculates that the shyness could simply be a strategy to reduce stimulation in relationships.

Dr. Aron described how some people (both HSP and non-HSP) are high sensation seekers (HSS) who enjoy stimulating activities, take risks, and are easily bored (2001). Challenges in relationships can arise when an HSP who needs low sensation is married to a non-HSP who is a high sensation seeker. The HSP in this case enjoys spending quiet time at home or alone while the non-HSP becomes bored with such a lifestyle, always craving stimulating activities. In her work on HSPs in relationships, Dr. Aron emphasizes the need for HSPs and non-HSPs to learn to compromise for the relationship to be successful. Both partners have to create optimal levels of arousal for the relationship to work, as well as employ creative solutions. Aron also emphasizes the importance of couples learning to accept each other's differences rather than blaming the other for having a different temperament.

However, even HSPs who are in a relationship with other HSPs have certain challenges (Aron 2001). They can both spend too much time in solitude and over-reacting to each other's sensitivities. HSP couples need to create more stimulation in their lives by pushing themselves to go out more since it helps a relationship to be participating in new, exciting adventures. However, HSP couples need to be careful not to spend too much time focusing on the problems of stimulation when on outings. For example, my HSP friend Nandita and I are quite compatible when we travel since she also insists on a quiet place to stay and abhors noise. However, when we traveled in stimuli-saturated India, we spent an inordinate amount of time discussing the noisy environment. By focusing on our common HSP concerns, we sometimes missed out on experiencing some of the spectacular sights of India.

Coupled HSPs need to deal with their differences in temperament or serious problems can arise. The HSP who does not work on creative solutions in relationships can get bogged down in daily conflicts with not only their partner, but with people in the non-HSP culture.

The Physiological Changes of Becoming Upset

When you become upset with someone, chemical changes occur in your body. When you are feeling resentment and frustration, stress hormones activate the central nervous system and you eventually become habituated to increased muscle tension, heart rate, and blood pressure. In addition, the stress hormone *catecholamine* (adrenaline-like hormone) is released during acute anger. When you experience chronic anger and frustration during the day, there is an excess of cortisol, a hormone that increases agitation, and a decrease of serotonin, which calms you down (Bhat 1995). An excess of catecholamine can create anxiety, apprehension, and fear. In addition, catecholamine speeds up the heart and can cause cardiac problems. An excess of cortisol leads to increased vigilance and a restless mind. You experience an exaggerated startle response, sounds appear louder, and lights seem brighter. During chronic anger and frustration, low levels of serotonin make it much harder to feel happy and fulfilled, which can lead to depression. Concurrently, the endorphins that create a sense of joy literally dry up, resulting in poor relationships with people.

When you let yourself become upset with "insensitive" people, you are only hurting yourself. These other people may not even know that you're angry with them. One of the greatest benefits of being an HSP is your ability to feel compassion deeply. You can use your innate kindness to open your heart to discourteous people and overcome hurt feelings. The Buddha said that using hatred to answer hatred only leads to an escalation of hatred. Mahatma Gandhi stated that if we follow the belief of an eye for an eye and a tooth for a tooth, the entire world would be blind and toothless. So open up your compassionate HSP heart to heal your relationships.

The following is a simple exercise that can easily transform detrimental feelings of anger into love.

Heart-Centered Visualization

Think of a recent experience when you felt hurt by another person and became angry. Is your attention focused in your head or heart? Now breathe deeply and slowly into your belly . . . Focus on the air filling your abdomen and slowly exhale . . . Now shift your awareness to the left hand . . . left elbow . . . left shoulder . . . left side of chest into your heart . . . Feel your heart expanding with love . . . Deeply experience the peace and harmony in the stillness and calmness of being centered in your heart . . . Next visualize a positive experience that you've had with the same person . . . How did you feel toward that person then? Take plenty of time to really visualize their good qualities . . . Ask yourself, can you let go of the anger? . . . Will you let go of the anger? . . . When will you let go of the anger? . . . The heart knows only love and will always let go of anger . . . Keep returning to the heart until you have released the anger . . . Once you have released the anger, you have shifted from a head-centered judgmental framework to heart-centered, caring love.

The next time that you're upset with someone that you have a relationship with, try utilizing this effective heart-centered visualization (Bhat 1995) and notice how quickly you can heal the rift.

Conflict Resolution for the HSP

In this section you will learn numerous methods to resolve conflicts with other people. As you read this part, jot down the techniques that you intuitively feel will help you the most. As you begin implementing the suggestions, you'll notice that your sensitivity may actually help you create more harmonious relationships.

Once-a-Week Mediation Program

One method of improving relationships that many of my students have had success with is what I call the "once-a-week mediation program" (Zeff 1999). Both partners agree not to discuss contentious issues during the week. When people fight with each other on a daily basis, the relationship begins to deteriorate. Unless the issue can be resolved immediately, both partners should choose a specific time during the week to discuss the problem. Pick a time when you will both be relaxed and not under any time constraints; for example, on a weekend afternoon. During the week you may write down everything that disturbs you about the other person. By writing down your feelings, you are not repressing your emotions or escalating the conflict by getting stuck in a daily verbal battle.

It is good for both partners to meditate or do some slow, deep breathing before discussing a controversial subject. Begin the session by telling the other person the ways that you appreciate your partner. Both parties should agree to speak in a soft voice, since HSPs do not respond well to loud noises. During the mediation session, tell the other person how you *feel* rather than enumerating all the ways that the other person is wrong for doing things differently or having a different temperament. Try to see the situation from the other person's perspective and be open to compromise. If you still can't resolve the issue, you may want to see a counselor.

Pause for Five Seconds

In chapter 3 we discussed the "pause for five seconds" technique to reduce stimulating arguments (Zeff 1999). Both parties agree to pause for five seconds before responding to each other. You may want to remind the other person that HSPs need more time to process information. It's very difficult for a conflict to escalate when both parties agree to wait five seconds before responding.

Nancy, a married HSP in her thirties, told me that she and her non-HSP husband, Rick, seemed to get into bitter disagreements where they both end up blaming each other. The arguments would keep escalating until Nancy would finally retreat into her room behind a locked door to get some relief from the overstimulating interaction. Their relationship had been deteriorating for several years and she recognized that her two young children suffered from witnessing the daily conflicts.

Nancy told me that at first Rick wasn't interested in waiting five seconds before responding when they began arguing. However, he finally said that he was willing to try anything to minimize the tension at home. Nancy reported that the first time they tried the technique, they noticed how inane the argument had been. After some time of practicing long pauses, they both actually started laughing. This process is a very effective tool for maintaining harmonious relationships—the pause that refreshes the HSP.

The 1 Percent Apology

Another method that I have frequently recommended to assuage disagreement, I call "the 1 percent apology" (Zeff 1999). In every conflict, there are always two sides to a story. Take responsibility for your part in the argument, even if you believe it's only 1 percent of the problem, and simply apologize. Your expression of remorse gives an opening for the other person to apologize for their part in the disagreement. However, even if you have to swallow some pride and the other person doesn't apologize, you have created peace of mind for yourself by opening your heart, not blaming anyone, and taking responsibility for your actions.

I remember when a non-HSP colleague began screaming at me for being five minutes late for an appointment. He began a voluminous tirade on the need for punctuality and how my tardiness ruined his experimental project. As an HSP, I was very hurt by his harsh outburst and fantasized how I would never subject myself to that person's rude behavior. I had decided never to work with this colleague again.

However, the following day I decided to apologize for being a few minutes late for the appointment. My associate immediately apologized for overreacting, informing me that he was having a very difficult day. If I hadn't apologized for my small part in the conflict, our professional association might have ended and the tension between us would have escalated.

Silence is Golden, and Talking Can Tarnish the Metal

Since the HSP feels more peaceful in a quiet environment, it's important that we reduce the amount of time we spend in mindless talking. Being in silence with people also lessens the potential for interpersonal conflicts. As mentioned in chapter 2, practicing silence is not for the shy and quiet HSP, but for those who tend to be loquacious. Excessive talking can be jarring to your nervous system when you have to constantly give your opinion or defend yourself. In addition, too much talking may deplete your energy level. It's important to choose your words carefully to avoid overstimulation.

Being in silence in a group setting can be very beneficial. You will feel more peaceful when you practice being quiet in large groups since you won't have to constantly state your opinions, ask unnecessary questions, or talk about yourself. If you are introverted in groups, this practice is not meant for you. Don't use silence as an excuse to avoid interpersonal connections, since the goal is to create a balanced life.

Allison was brought up in a large family with five brothers and sisters and told me one night after class that she really dreaded her family functions because of all the constant arguing and noise. She would invariably get drawn into contentious familial fights and leave the event feeling drained and anxious. I suggested that she simply try being in silence during the upcoming Thanksgiving dinner at her parent's home. A few weeks later Allison told me that it was the first time that she had left a family function feeling peaceful. She simply told her family that she loved them, but was trying to talk less. No one wanted to attack her since she wasn't responding, and Allison felt really safe at a family function for the first time. At first it may feel strange being in silence with people, but as you experience more joy during such quiet interludes, you will want to integrate this practice into more areas of your life. It may be a good idea to ask your family and friends to remind you to be in silence to reinforce this practice.

HSP Assertiveness Training, 101

Since our aggressive society values non-HSP behavior, HSPs must learn to create boundaries and speak up. Unfortunately, many HSPs are shy and feel embarrassed to state what they want. Since you may have been told throughout your life that there was something wrong with you for being sensitive, you may suffer in silence or try to control the environment by withdrawing from difficult situations. However, if you repress your feelings, you can create frustration, isolation, and depression. When you practice asserting yourself from a loving place, you can make positive changes in all your relationships. The other person may be unaware that their behavior is irritating you. If you wait until the person behind you on the airplane has been kicking the back of your seat for a half-hour, you will tend to overreact when you finally ask them to stop their annoying habit.

It's helpful to make a personal connection with someone before you request that they change their behavior. In some situations it can be useful to state that you have a finely tuned nervous system before you request that the person change their behavior.

A few months ago, I had to ask a non-HSP neighbor to be more quiet. I live in a building where the doors tend to slam shut, making a loud noise. I began the conversation by asking how his Thanksgiving holiday had been and what his plans for Christmas were. I then explained that I have a finely tuned nervous system that makes me very sensitive to loud noises. Next, I said that I would greatly appreciate it if he could please close his door a little more slowly when he leaves his apartment. Finally, I thanked him for his kind consideration and asked if I could help him in anyway.

In this particular case, the neighbor acquiesced to my request, making my life a lot calmer. However, sometimes you may deal with less accommodating people who may resent your asking them to close their door slowly. You may need to come up with some creative solutions, such as helping install a device to stop the door from slamming.

However, if the person reacts in a hostile manner, you may have to make changes in your lifestyle, such as using a white noise machine or spending less time in the noisiest room. In an extreme instance consider moving if you cannot deal with the situation. Many years ago, a neighbor below my bedroom used to slam his door shut at 4 A.M. every morning on his way to work, startling me awake. After much fruitless negotiation with the tenant and the landlord, I finally solved the problem by sleeping in the living room and making my bedroom into an office.

One HSP student, Patricia, mentioned that sometimes it's more prudent to surrender to minor temporary inconveniences than to assert yourself. When Patricia was at the movies some people in front of her started talking. From past experience she realized that sometimes people who talk a lot at the movies tend to react defensively when they are asked to be quiet. She also had some fear of confronting, however gently, this bellicose group of people. Instead of immediately asking the people to be quiet, she decided to wait to see if the chatting would subside. Since the talking became less frequent, Patricia decided not to ask the people to be quiet. She mentioned that she could have moved her seat if the noise became intolerable or reported the loud patrons to the manager.

Heart-Centered Assertion

To enhance your ability to speak up, you may want to take an assertiveness training class, discuss this issue with a therapist, or role-play the situation with a friend. Try the following guided visualization before asserting what you want.

> Breathe slowly and deeply into your belly for a few moments
> . . . Focus your attention on your heart . . . Visualize telling the
> offending person what you want from your heart . . . Notice
> that the person is unaware of how their behavior is affecting
> you . . . If this is someone you have a relationship with, imagine
> telling the person that you have a finely tuned nervous system
> . . . Then envision politely asking the person to change their
> behavior . . . Now clearly observe the person making the
> positive change . . .

When we assert ourselves from a loving and nonjudgmental place, there is an excellent probability that we will make positive changes in our life.

Forgiveness: The Key to Inner-Peace

Many great teachers have said forgiveness is the key to good physical and emotional health. How can you be healthy and happy if you're stuck in a position of anger and blame (Hay 1987)? If you're blaming someone then you become a victim, and victims can't be emotionally or physically healthy. Louise Hay, author of *You Can Heal Your Life*, has written that you can literally eat away the cells of your own body with resentment (1987). When you forgive others, you set yourself free and give yourself the greatest gift of all: peace and joy. It's hard for people to forgive others when they truly believe in the atavistic philosophy of an eye for an eye. When you forgive someone, you are not approving of someone's poor behavior, but freeing yourself. Besides, everyone is doing the best they can given the knowledge that they have at that particular time.

One HSP student, Ellen, told me that she became very upset when her husband divorced her, and due to her sensitivity, she stayed stuck feeling depressed and angry for a very long time. However, after practicing specific forgiveness exercises daily for many months, she was finally able to release her anger toward her ex-husband and subsequently felt much better.

It also becomes easier to forgive people who hurt us when we can feel empathy for someone who is so disturbed that they would want to seriously harm another person. I've noticed that sometimes people are unable to forgive because they don't want to give up the need to be abused. Sometimes HSPs who have been shamed as children don't want to let go of their emotional pain because they have become so attached and used to it. Remember that when you are out of balance, you may tend to crave more emotional pain, which can then create further disharmonious relationships. Since emotional pain cannot simultaneously survive in a state of joy, the more we choose to implement techniques such as forgiveness, the more our interpersonal relationships will improve.

Healing Low Self-Esteem

You may not need to forgive quite so much if you could include fewer contentious or insensitive people in your life. One way to attract fewer of these people and help yourself deal better with the ones around you is to increase your self-esteem. Louise Hay has written that if you repeat the affirmation "I love and approve of myself exactly as I am" five hundred times a day, you will be able to heal your interpersonal relationships (1987). Since feelings of inadequacy are based on a belief that you're not good enough, when you affirm that you are perfect exactly as you are, your self-esteem rises. As an HSP, you have been frequently told that you are not worthwhile since you haven't measured up to the false, non-HSP value system. Just like a tape recorder that plays back what is recorded, every thought you think and every word you speak reinforces your beliefs and helps create your future (Hay 1987). When you constantly affirm that you love and approve of yourself exactly as you are, you will gain self-confidence and improve your relationships with others.

Many years ago I tried repeating this self-accepting affirmation. I would look into the mirror daily and state "I love and approve of myself exactly as I am" hundreds of times. When I was driving in the car I would repeat the affirmation as I smiled at people passing me on the highway. I even repeated the affirmation when I played basketball, especially if I missed a shot. After just a few weeks of repeating the affirmation, my life changed for the better. My relationships with people improved, my self-confidence grew and I began to accept my sensitivity.

Investigate Your Thoughts

When HSPs are constantly engaged in a futile battle, fighting the reality of living in our non-HSP world, stress and tension develop. Have you noticed that when you get upset, it is usually because you're unwilling to accept reality? Byron Katie, author of *Loving What Is*, has created a simple, yet effective method of self-inquiry that helps create harmonious relationships (2002). She recommends investigating your judgments about people by asking four questions: Is it true? Can I really know that it's true? How do I react when I believe a negative thought about someone, which may not even be true? How would I treat the person if I dropped the judgmental belief? The final step is to turn the equation around by replacing the person you feel resentment toward with your name. For example, "My husband should understand me" becomes "I should understand my husband."

Through this process you can learn that you don't really meet anyone new, but just keep encountering the same story with everyone whom you meet. It's all about projection, the psychological phenomenon of attributing your own qualities, either positive or negative, to other people. Due to projection, when you love yourself, you love the world and when you hate yourself you hate the world. When you're feeling good about yourself, your relationships improve but when your self-esteem is low, you experience more interpersonal tension.

It can help your self-esteem when you realize that whenever anyone judges you for being sensitive, it really has nothing to do with you. Other people's opinion of you is actually none of your business since they are simply projecting their judgments. Likewise, when you get upset with someone else, it usually has more to do with your belief system and less to do with the other person's behavior.

When you can own the quality in yourself that you don't like in the other person, you can release your judgments. One HSP student in her fifties, Jessica, told the class that an insensitive non-HSP coworker yelled at her for making a mistake on a project at work. Jessica reported that she was so angry at this coworker that she told everyone at her job about the colleague's hostile behavior. She had become obsessed with the coworker's behavior and had thousands of angry thoughts about her. When she investigated her thoughts and actions, Jessica realized that the coworker had expressed anger toward her only once while Jessica had exhibited rage about the colleague thousands of times. Jessica was shocked to realize that she was repeating the same type of hostile behavior that she detested in the coworker.

As an HSP, it is prudent not to falsely anticipate the worst in non-HSPs. For example, I once rented a car in Manhattan. The rental agent I dealt with appeared unscrupulous. He demanded in an abrasive voice, "Ya got a credit card?" As he puffed on his smelly cigar he continued, "I don't rent to nobody without no credit card." He then screamed at another customer, "I told ya to park da car on the street, not in dis here lot."

Since I'd heard that small rental companies in New York like to rip off customers, I believed that the agent would try to illegally charge me for an extra day for the rental. During the four-hour trip back to Manhattan, I visualized different scenarios as to how I would confront this dishonest clerk. With every mile I drove, I became more incensed at the audacity of the agent who was trying to steal my money. When I pulled into the parking lot, I was ready for battle. When I entered the office, the same insensitive salesman with the big cigar looked up at me and asked if everything went okay. He checked the car and mileage and surprisingly said, "Thanks," as he handed me my receipt for the correct number of days. What, no battle? I was shocked to realize that I had created an entire story that wasn't true. The lies that were arising in my mind were the only dishonest aspects in the rental transaction (Zeff 2002). Perhaps I should buy a bumper sticker that reads, "Don't believe your thoughts."

While your sensitive nervous system may cause you to overreact to hurtful comments, it's your mind that perpetuates the frustration. If you see potential problems everywhere, you are like someone in a dark room who is fighting their own shadow. But when you finally turn on the light, you realize that there's no one else there. You were just fighting yourself.

Be a Witness to Your Thoughts

As we have just discussed, identification with thoughts in your mind can perpetuate interpersonal problems. If you can step back and just observe the thoughts and emotions rather than immediately reacting, more harmonious relationships will manifest. When you find yourself obsessing about how someone hurt you, simply step back and watch the thought. Just note how the ego/mind continues judging others, resulting in emotional pain and strife for you as well as the other person (Tolle 1999). As you remove yourself from being an active participant in the conflict in your mind, ask yourself what the next thought will be. When that thought has arisen, just inquire what the next thought will be. As you begin to observe the thoughts float by without attaching to them, you begin to realize that you are more than the myriad of negative thoughts racing through your mind.

As you observe your thoughts in the present moment, you can let go of remorse over the past and worries about the future (Tolle 1999). The ego/mind thrives on conflict in order to survive. Emotional pain needs food to continue growing and negative thoughts are just the nourishment it needs to get stronger. However, as you begin to listen deeply and with awareness to a negative thought in the present moment, the painful thought subsides and loses power. You have ceased to energize the mind by identifying with it. The negative thoughts *cannot* continue growing when you are focused in the present moment (Tolle 1999).

When we remain focused in the present moment, emotional pain evaporates. Janice, an HSP in her fifties, had been meditating for many years. She told the class about an incident at her job as a part-time teacher and how remaining focused in the present helped her. Janice's principal told her that, due to increased enrollment, she would have to teach extra classes for the same salary. She felt powerless and angry since her principal appeared quite inflexible. Janice had been sitting at her desk in the late afternoon unconsciously obsessing about her predicament and worrying about how she would meet her financial obligations. Suddenly she looked out the window and noticed the radiant, yellow leaves falling from a magnificent oak tree on the crisp, clear autumn day. Janice then gazed at the luminous sunlight streaming through her window before dusk. She closed her eyes and began focusing on different parts of her body as she felt a peaceful energy flowing through her body. When a pessimistic thought about her dilemma arose, she just observed the negative thought about the past or future and returned to the present. Janice then opened her eyes and savored the natural beauty outside her window. As she remained in the present moment, all the emotional pain about her job predicament simply dissolved.

Although the mind constantly releases incessant, pessimistic thoughts about the past and future, there is a power within you that is always able to dissolve the negativity and experience the bliss of the present. When you find yourself thinking about a painful interaction with someone, simply observe whether you are in the past or the future. Observe your resistance to letting go of the pain and your attachment to it. Notice that as soon as you become focused in the present moment, the pain dissolves and you feel peaceful. Remember, "now" spelled backwards is "won."

Active Listening Diminishes Pain

Frequently when relationships become antagonistic, neither party is really listening to the other person. Instead of listening, you may begin thinking of ways to deal with the emotional pain that you are experiencing. You may not hear a word that the "offending" party says as you wait for an opportunity to express your hurt.

When you actively listen to the other person, the conflict usually disappears. The next time that you're in an argument, conduct the following experiment: focus all your attention on the person you're talking to for just five minutes, without interjecting your opinion or sharing your personal experiences. Simply reflect back the feeling or content of what the person is saying from a caring place in your heart. Also, listen to the deeper needs behind the words to really tune into what the person wants.

Active listening can feel phony to the other person if you are doing it as a technique without genuinely caring about what the other person is saying. When I first began working as a family therapist, I mechanically reflected what a teenage client was saying during our sessions. Finally, the boy stood up and walked out, remarking that if I started talking like a parrot again, he wasn't coming back. Yet if you genuinely listen to and reflect what the other person is saying, the argument usually ends, since everyone really wants to be heard. It's also beneficial to ask the other person to listen deeply to you, which will help you feel acknowledged.

Observe how often you talk about yourself, as opposed to tuning into what the other person is saying during a conversation. When you become self-centered, you can create negative emotions that can culminate in frustrating interpersonal relationships. Self-indulgent, negative emotions actually increase stress hormones. However, when you are really interested in listening to the other person, endorphins may be secreted, creating inner peace. Therefore, the more time you spend listening deeply to people, the more your relationships will improve and the better you will feel both emotionally and physically.

As a highly sensitive person, it may not be easy to listen carefully to the other person when you have been hurt. However, when you remain calm and centered instead of reacting, it will be easier to resolve a conflict. If you interrupt the other person or respond in a judgmental manner, the contentious interaction only escalates. The next time you feel hurt during an argument, stop and center yourself by taking a few slow, deep breaths. When you are calm and centered, you will be better prepared for active listening instead of reactive squabbling.

Smile and the World Smiles with You

As an HSP, your sensitivity can make you take things too seriously in your relationships with people. It's impossible to stay in an argument when both parties are laughing and smiling with each other. When you keep your sense of humor, you will become happier. As you smile, you release endorphins that make you feel peaceful (Bhat 1995). Norman Cousins believed in the healing power of humor. Many years ago he actually healed a catastrophic illness through laughter. He would engage in humorous activities, such as renting funny Marx Brothers movies, so that he would laugh out loud (1983). You can literally laugh yourself to wellness.

Interestingly, the enzyme d-lysozyme is secreted when you laugh so deeply that you shed tears. Research indicates that this enzyme actually boosts the immune system (Bhat 1995). In all stages of smiling, the anal sphincter contracts and relaxes. However, when you're frowning, the internal anal sphincter gets very tight, which is a cue for sympathetic arousal that actually creates constipation. Perhaps laughter will be sold one day as the ultimate laxative.

Having a sense of humor is more than just telling jokes, but also being open to experiencing peace and joy. Usually, a lack of humor relates to an inflexible view of the world. Children smile and laugh four hundred times a day, whereas for adults it's only fifteen times or less (Bhat 1995). Since it takes seventy-five muscles to frown and only fifteen muscles to smile, recapturing the joy of childhood can be relatively effortless.

When I become too serious, I reflect on life's absurdities. Whenever I have felt overwhelmed trying to meet a deadline on this book about how to create inner-peace, I would break out in a big smile and frequently end up laughing at the irony. Laughter is a marvelous medicine that puts problems in perspective. What are some ludicrous paradoxes in your life that can make you laugh out loud?

When there was a lot of tension with my son when he was younger, I would frequently dress up like a frumpy clown and make bizarre noises, making us both howl with laughter. You may want to develop your sense of humor by engaging in some of the following: rent funny movies, go to the library or a bookstore to obtain humorous books, tickle your partner, make funny faces in a mirror, and play silly games with children. Don't forget to smile a lot.

It's also beneficial for HSPs to be able to laugh at their sensitivity. Did you hear the story about the HSP who joined the army and saved his entire company from certain death from the enemy? As soon as the noisy bombs began exploding he led a retreat to safety and won a medal for bravery.

Heal the World, Heal Yourself

One of the finest aspects of being an HSP is your ability to feel compassion for suffering humanity. Obsessing about how someone has hurt your feelings only makes the situation worse. You can transform these lingering negative feelings by showing kindness and compassion toward others. If you perform acts of kindness, you would be using your innate sensitivity to heal yourself as well as the world. Let your service to those in need create sparks of love in your heart and throughout the world. You can use your compassionate heart to transcend your interpersonal conflicts by engaging in some of the following activities: make a meal for an elderly neighbor; volunteer to help at a homeless shelter; play a game with a lonely child; visit patients in a nursing home; do your partner or housemate's chores; say a kind word to the harried sales clerk; let the driver in the other car go in front of you. What are some other acts of kindness that you can do today?

When you perform kind acts, you not only uplift others, but you transcend negative, self-centered emotions. The law of karma states that whatever energy you put out comes back to you. When you dwell on interpersonal problems due to your sensitivity, you may feel depressed; but when you perform kind deeds by helping others, the endorphins that are released in your body will literally make you feel joyful. When you reach out to a stranger, that person may just be a potential friend that you have not yet met.

Recently at a community meal, I was sitting at a table with some friends enjoying a pleasant conversation, when out of the corner of my eye I saw a bandaged man dressed in disheveled clothes looking for a place to sit. As I looked closer, I noticed that there was yellow pus and blood staining the large bandage covering his chin. My instinctual reaction was to make sure he didn't sit down in the empty seat next to mine, so I purposely turned away hoping that he would sit somewhere else. My strategy worked as he sat down by himself at the table behind mine. During a lull in the conversation, I again noticed this sad and lonely looking man hunched over his meal.

I couldn't bear to avoid the pathetic looking man anymore so I turned around and introduced myself. Suddenly, a bright smile appeared on his scarred face as I asked him to join us. He told me that he had cancer that had spread to different parts of his body and that the tumor on his chin was draining. He said that he was hesitant to come to the community gathering since everyone had been avoiding him recently due to his physical disability. However, the ailing man, my friends, and I all left the gathering feeling uplifted due to the meaningful connection that was established.

As an HSP you may sometimes have to overcome your innate desire to avoid stimulation in order to help those in need. Since HSPs frequently know what needs to be done in emergency situations, you may want to occasionally risk some personal emotional trauma for the betterment of humanity. Ann, an HSP who tends to faint at the sight of blood and is easily disturbed by violence, witnessed a horrific automobile accident as she was driving on her street. She pulled her car over and had to decide what to do. Ann realized that witnessing the trauma would adversely affect her. However, as a compassionate person she felt that she must help the injured people even if she experienced some negative emotions.

When Ann crossed the street she noticed that both cars were severely damaged. She helped calm one frantic driver who was standing outside of her car crying. The other driver was stuck in her car screaming that her back hurt and that she couldn't move. Ann found herself in the unlikely role of an emergency medical technician. Ann gently held the injured woman's hand and talked to her, trying to alleviate her panic until the ambulance arrived. Although Ann was deeply shaken by the experience, she felt a deep sense of satisfaction for stopping to help the victims of the accident.

It's virtually impossible to spend time obsessing about how someone has hurt your feelings when you're focused on serving humanity. *Ryan's Well* (Cook 2001) is a story of how a highly sensitive Canadian boy named Ryan Hreljac became very upset when he learned a few years ago, as a first grader, that thousands of African children die every year from drinking contaminated water. Due to his sensitivity, compassion, and willpower, this little six-year-old boy single-handedly raised enough money to create wells in Africa. As a result of his effort many children were spared from drinking contaminated water.

I want to share an inspiring e-mail I recently received from Ryan:

Hi Ted,

Hi, it's just me, Ryan, and my mom, Susan! I wanted to thank you for your e-mail all the way from California. I have many things planned for 2004. I promise to keep working to help raise money for clean water. Maybe, if everyone works together, one day there will be peace and clean water for everyone! Thanks again! I hope my dreams come true, and I hope your dreams come true too!

Well, thanks again for writing, and remember you can do anything but only if you really try hard and you really want to!

Ryan and Susan (Typist/Mom) Hreljac

Like Ryan, you can choose to use your sensitivity to help alleviate suffering humanity or you can use your sensitivity to focus on your hurt feelings.

Spiritualize Your Relationships

Your relationships can become more harmonious when you create a spiritual connection with others. Instead of wasting precious moments arguing about sensitivity differences, consider new activities that are fun and uplifting for all concerned. Take a spiritually uplifting walk in nature with your partner, family, and friends. As you stroll along a park trail together, savor the beauty of a bluebird landing on the branch of a flowering dogwood tree, or notice a squirrel scampering through the lush, green grass. You feel serene as you gaze into the eyes of your companions in this tranquil setting, as your souls merge into a divine, peaceful state.

You may also want to spend some time each day performing regular spiritual practices with your family and friends. These spiritual methods could include meditating, praying, reading an inspiring book, or watching an uplifting movie. When you have a spiritual practice that you can do with those you love, the soul connection grows stronger, making it easier to transcend petty temperament differences.

Partners who engage in enjoyable activities together have less frequent arguments. Since HSPs thrive in calm, natural environments, it's quite beneficial to arrange outings to the ocean, rivers, mountains, or forests. However, when HSPs are involved in overstimulating activities like eating out in large, noisy restaurants, the spiritual connection can be stifled. It's important to compromise with your non-HSP family members and friends when planning activities. While it's all right to occasionally push yourself to be in stimulating environments for small periods of time, try not to go beyond your threshold to placate your non-HSP family and friends.

We are all souls who have taken a temporary human body to learn certain lessons. When you relate to another on a soul level instead of on a transitory personality level, your relationships will improve. Inside the most insensitive and vulgar person is hidden a lotus blossom of love waiting to bud. When you nurture the divine qualities in other people by spreading kindness, the flower of higher consciousness will bloom in all your relationships.

It's important to feel compassion for less sensitive people. You don't want to become an "insensitive" sensitive person. While the non-HSP tolerance may be higher for loud noises, strong smells, and bright lights, they also can experience tension when they are overstimulated.

Xenophobia (the fear of what is strange or different) can create internal wars within us, as well as larger international wars. However, the more you practice feeling a sense of unity with others, the more your judgments lessen and your positive spiritual connection with everyone increases. If you accidentally poke your eye with your finger, you will comfort both your finger and your eye. You won't blame your finger (Amritaswarupananda 1989). Likewise, when you experience your divine connection with all sentient beings, you will want to always help others as you would yourself.

You can also experience a spiritual connection with your pets. Many studies have documented the healing affect that pets have on people (Becker 2002). For example, depressed patients in nursing homes respond positively to visits by dogs as they receive the animals' unconditional love. A loving, nurturing pet is exactly what most sensitive people need as an antidote to the stress of living in a competitive, non-HSP world.

One of my students, Jane, told me that ten years ago she was diagnosed with cancer and had been given five months to live. She described how her dogs would nuzzle up to her when she was in pain. She felt that on a subtle level, the dogs actually absorbed her pain. She credits the unconditional love and loyalty she received from her beloved pets as the reason she is still alive today.

Older and Wiser

In our Cinderella society most people are conditioned to believe that they will only be content if they live happily ever after with the perfect soul mate. In spite of the fact that many marriages end in divorce or are frequently unhappy, most people still cling to the false belief that their happiness is solely dependent on having a loving, intimate relationship with a partner. However, as we learn our life lessons, we can begin to look inside for inner peace.

Harmonious relationships don't just happen. They take a lot of work. Sometimes, no matter what techniques you try to improve your relationships, they just don't work out. However, once you work on changing *yourself*, your relationships will improve. Once you increase your self-esteem and become more peaceful, you'll lessen any temptation to bring belligerent people into your life and will attract more loving people.

There was a great spiritual teacher who adopted the name Peace Pilgrim to symbolize her life's work. As an elderly woman, she walked alone throughout North America for thirty years promoting peace. That whole time, she was never accosted (Peace Pilgrim 1994). When she was asked why no one ever bothered her, she responded that she would look at people with the deepest feelings of love, as she believed in the goodness inside of everyone. I think Peace Pilgrim would agree that the most important factor that determines harmony in relationships is your inner-state of peace and love.

Creating Harmonious Relationships

- Spend time every day in silence with your partner, family, and friends.

- Both parties in a relationship can agree to discuss conflict only once a week. You can write down all your grievances about the other person throughout the week, and save any conflict discussion until the appointed time.

- Both parties agree to pause for five seconds before responding during a disagreement.

- Take responsibility for your behavior. Instead of blaming others, apologize for your part in a disagreement, even if it's 1 percent.

- Investigate negative thoughts about other people that arise to see if they are really true. Your mind may make up negative stories about people to confirm your belief system, resulting in contentious relationships.

- Practice living in the present moment.

- When you're upset with someone you know well, try focusing your awareness in your heart, visualizing a positive experience you've had with the person until you can release the negative feelings.

- Utilize the technique of active listening.

- Practice forgiveness of others as well as yourself.

- Be a witness to any negative thoughts about people. Just ask yourself what the next thought will be as you simply observe the thoughts arise and disappear.

- Keep your sense of humor. Smile a lot.

- Rather than silently fuming, learn ways to assert yourself in a kind manner.

- Plan positive activities with your friends and family: Spend time in nature, meditate together, enjoy a creative project.

- Use your compassion to focus on helping your family, friends, and society.

- Be aware of your unity with all beings, especially with pets, nature, and your connection to the Divine.

———————— *7* ————————

Creating a Peaceful
Work Environment

$\mathcal{I}$n this chapter you will learn how to reduce stress at work while creating a relaxed job environment. It is challenging for sensitive people to work under time pressure for an inconsiderate boss or with difficult colleagues. Over 95 percent of the HSPs that I surveyed stated that stress at work affects their physical or emotional health.

Work Stress: Public and Personal Costs

In an interview with Dr. Paul Rosch, president of the American Institute of Stress on November 10, 2003, one million American workers are absent daily due to stress. Stress at work is estimated to cost industry in the United States a staggering $300 billion a year in absenteeism, injuries, and disease!

Due to your conscientiousness and desire to fulfill your obligations at work, you may find yourself frantically multitasking, to complete arduous assignments, resulting in emotional and physical burnout. Even in less overwhelming situations, your desire to be conscientious and not make mistakes can create stress. The feeling of not being able to live up to the non-HSP, Type A work standards can create frustration, anxiety, and low self-esteem for the HSP.

Some stressful job conditions can be ameliorated if you work with a supportive staff. There is a correlation between job satisfaction and positive social interactions at work (Dalai Lama 2003). Depersonalization at work is a major cause of both stress and unhappiness on the job. The lack of real human contact at work (sometimes we're more likely to e-mail the person in the next cubicle than stand up and talk to them) contributes to a feeling of anomie in the workplace.

When you are performing work that you feel is meaningful, your job satisfaction increases. For example, if you can understand how your job is benefiting humanity, you will likely become more enthusiastic about your vocation.

In our materialistic society, even HSPs may adopt the belief that making more money—even at the cost of your physical, emotional, and spiritual well being—is worth it. Once your basic needs have been met, you may sometimes still drive yourself to earn more and more money, believing that external remuneration will bring inner-happiness. Studies show that there is no correlation between happiness in life and increased income once your basic needs have been met (Dalai Lama 2003).

HSPs need a lot of downtime and may find it difficult to work a forty-hour week. Unfortunately, many American jobs require employees to work overtime. Most Americans annually work several weeks longer than both French and Germans. Given this out-of-balance American work ethic, HSPs have to create their own, unique job schedule or risk being caught up in an overwhelming work situation.

Our Attitude about Work

Attitude is an important factor in job satisfaction. When you perceive your work from a global perspective, you can gain new appreciation for your occupation. People in developing countries and even laborers in our own country may perform heavy physical work for more than ten hours a day for a fraction of your salary. Many unemployed people would jump at the chance to work in your field. Suddenly, that "boring" job may seem a lot more interesting.

If you are dissatisfied with your work, investigate the cause of your dissatisfaction. Is it due to the unreasonable demands of a disrespectful boss? Are coworkers rude to you throughout the day? Or is your frustration due to an internal pattern of not being satisfied with most aspects of your life? We usually bring our beliefs and attitudes into the workplace so that our job mirrors our life. The mind always thinks the grass is greener somewhere else, and the ego thrives on conflict to maintain its separate identity.

My dad was one of the few people I have known who absolutely loved his job. He worked as a community social worker, organizing Jewish nonprofit agencies for more than fifty years. He continued working as a consultant and supervising social-work students well into his late eighties. His enthusiasm and positive attitude were two important elements that created his high degree of job satisfaction. And, of course, he was naturally a positive and enthusiastic man outside of work, taking that attitude to work every day. Another factor that created his love for his profession was that he passionately believed that he was helping those in need, such as the elderly, immigrants, and those with physical and emotional problems. He found special meaning in an assignment, working in Europe rebuilding the Jewish community that was nearly destroyed by the holocaust.

Even a tedious job becomes meaningful and fun when you develop a positive attitude and work with supportive people. Derrick, a single man in his early twenties, works in a warehouse that ships medical equipment to countries in Asia. He found that categorizing medical supplies by himself was so boring that he was going to quit the job after the first week. However, during his second week he was assigned an enthusiastic coworker who pointed out how each piece of equipment would help heal a sick person. The other employee made jokes as they listened to uplifting music. Derrick's entire attitude changed, and he began to enjoy his job so much that he willingly worked overtime on some occasions.

While it's easier for a non-HSP to cope with heavy job responsibilities, once you develop the qualities of acceptance and surrender, it will be easier for you to function at work. In chapter 2 I described a postal employee who became overwhelmed daily as he sorted letters, while the CEO of a major corporation stated that his job wasn't stressful at all. The CEO didn't worry if a task wasn't completed. One HSP student told me that she became extremely upset if she felt that she made a mistake at work. She agonized for hours about the possible error. After working with her for several weeks, she slowly began to realize that all she could do was her best. She finally let go of her need to complete all tasks perfectly.

When I was a vocational rehabilitation counselor working with injured workers, I often knew during the first interview which clients would be successfully rehabilitated into a new job. Clients who blamed their employer and complained about their insurance company often created obstacles to their rehabilitation program. When clients had a positive attitude toward vocational rehabilitation and accepted their limitations without dwelling on their injury, they invariably obtained new, satisfying work.

The greater the will to overcome difficulties on the job, the better the probability of having a positive work experience. For example, when you make an effort to improve your relationships with people at work, your job satisfaction increases. However, if you put forth a great deal of energy to improve a difficult job situation and nothing works, you can always quit. You are never truly stuck.

Less Money, but More Happiness

It will increase your sense of well being to work in a less demanding job that may pay a lower salary but give you the freedom to spend more time pursuing enjoyable and calming activities (Dalai Lama 2003). On their deathbed, no one ever wished that they spent more time at the office making money. In the final analysis, the amount of love that we've shared with each other is the only thing that we will take with us when we leave our bodies.

Materialistic cravings create a vicious circle. The more money people make, the more money they think they need. The more ego gratification employees receive on the job, the more status they will crave. People who live in expensive, air conditioned houses still commit suicide (Amritaswarupananda 1989). What we really need to do is air condition our minds by investigating why we would continue to work in a very stressful job that is harming our physical, emotional, and spiritual well being.

If you make your job your entire life, you're setting yourself up for emotional trauma when you eventually leave the job or retire. It's better to live a balanced life, making time for a satisfying social life and pursuing interesting activities outside of work.

Amongst HSPs there is a wide range of work pressure and stimulation that we can handle. You have to find your own balance between working in a boring job and one that is too stressful. I know some high sensation seeking non-HSPs who thrive on work pressure in a high-paying job. It gives them an adrenalin rush to meet deadlines, similar to a football player making a touchdown against a formidable opponent. However, for highly sensitive people, the same work environment would most likely create a severe anxiety reaction.

Sometimes you may feel stuck in a difficult job situation. In reality, when you are open to new possibilities, your work situation always improves. Connie, one of my students, was a single, high-sensation-seeking HSP woman in her forties. She worked for a small company as an administrative assistant. Unfortunately, her boss continually increased her workload so that she ended up working six days a week from 8 A.M. to 7 P.M. and commuting an hour each way. Due to constant job stress, she developed anxiety and gastrointestinal problems.

Connie felt that she needed that salary to make her high mortgage payments and that there weren't any other well-paying jobs near her home. Connie told me that she grew up in a trailer and had always dreamed of living in a beautiful house. She would not consider moving. I recommended that she investigate whether she could find another well-paying job closer to home. After several weeks of encouraging her to look for another job, she reported that she actually found a job near her house working only forty hours a week that paid almost as much as her previous sixty-plus hour a week job.

How to Reduce Stress at Work

Many specific methods can help create a more peaceful work environment. Consider which of the suggestions in this section are germane to your workplace and try to incorporate some of the following ideas into your work situation.

You can listen to calming background music to reduce or eliminate ambient noise at work. Many HSPs have told me that they frequently listen to music, wearing a headset, while some wear earplugs on the job. Put up inspiring pictures of natural settings, such as land- or seascapes, or family pictures. If you are working under fluorescent lights or in an artificial, urban setting, gazing at nature will soothe your nerves. It may also help if you bring flowers and plants to your office. Your nervous system will be calmed by inhaling the delicate fragrance of flowers or by gazing at an exquisite bouquet. Surround yourself with love by bringing in pictures of family and friends. Make sure that you have a comfortable chair to sit in throughout the workday so that your muscles are relaxed. You can buy a massage cushion for your chair that will electronically massage your tension away throughout the day.

As I mentioned in chapter 3, try to transform the sound of the telephone ringing at work into a relaxation cue. First, lower the volume if possible. Let the ringing remind you to relax your muscles, take some slow deep breaths, and repeat a mantra such as "peace." If possible, don't answer the phone until the third or fourth ring. Use those few moments to relax deeply (Hanh 1991).

It's a good idea to create a daily work schedule to reduce stimulation, rather than immediately jumping into a busy workday every morning. When you first arrive at work, center yourself by spending a few moments either meditating or doing some slow, deep abdominal breathing. Look at your work schedule for the day and, given your sensitivity, decide on a realistic expectation of assignments to be completed. Try to schedule some time for relaxation breaks, and remember to practice progressive muscle relaxation at your workstation.

As we've seen, the HSP traits of being very responsible and feeling easily overwhelmed by time pressure can really exacerbate stress. If you feel that the demands of the day will be too overwhelming, try to scale down your workload or talk to your supervisor. Be realistic, and don't create added stress by trying to push yourself beyond your limits.

I have learned to say no to taking on extra commitments at work and in my personal life. Although I sometimes feel guilty when I say no, the alternative for me is increased anxiety, since I always feel that I need to follow through with any commitment that I make. However, if I feel that my energy is strong and I have free time, I will frequently volunteer on the spot to help out in areas that I previously didn't want to commit to. This method of spontaneously assisting others seems to suit the HSP temperament by employing the characteristic of compassion without feeling overwhelmed by future commitments.

Since HSPs are easily affected by other people's moods, when you're working with others under time pressure, you may write, talk, and type faster, which exacerbates tension. You may want to put a note on your desk reminding yourself to work slower rather than being swept away by the frenetic moods of your colleagues. You can remind your coworkers that Type A employees succeed in spite of their time urgent, competitive, and aggressive behavior, not because of it. Then pause to reflect that the trudging tortoise beats the hyper hare.

The use of aromatherapy, which is the inhalation of the fragrances of vaporized essential oils, is another effective method to create tranquility at work. The fragrance of certain essential oils have proven effective against stress and help create relaxation (Worwood 1997). For example, a study showed that keyboard errors decreased by over 50 percent when the fragrance of lemon is diffused into an office (Worwood 1997).

If you're sitting all day at work, it's important to periodically take walking or stretching breaks. The walking meditation described in chapter 2 can be an effective break. You can always do stretching, even while seated in your chair. Try to do progressive relaxation for a few moments every hour by visualizing all the muscles in your body relaxing further and further as you take some slow, deep breaths. I remember one student who worked in a very busy medical office and told me that she didn't have time to take even one break throughout the day. However, she tried using progressive relaxation while sitting at her desk and found it quite effective in reducing stress.

If you have clients or customers who come to your workplace, you may want to have some uplifting magazines available to create a peaceful environment. In addition, offering calming herb tea and healthy snacks like fruit is another potent method to create a tranquil work environment.

Some progressive, large companies have fitness centers and meditation rooms for their employees. You may want to investigate with your supervisor the possibility of creating a meditation room. You could point out that employee's efficiency would improve if they had a peaceful room to meditate in for short breaks during the day. A quiet, dark room is a godsend for the HSP who works in a stimulating environment.

To help increase harmony at work, recommend to your supervisor to install a suggestion box (Zeff 1999). Since the HSP may have many complaints and feel embarrassed to ask for changes, the anonymity of the suggestion box would be beneficial. The suggestion box could also give an opportunity for non-HSPs, who may be mildly bothered by some of the same conditions, to express their opinion.

HSPs with insomnia usually find it stressful to be at work early every morning. Ask your employer about the possibility of arriving at work later in exchange for taking a shorter lunch hour or working a little later in the day. One student told me that when he didn't have to be at work early every morning, he wouldn't have as much difficulty falling asleep. He would tell himself that he could always sleep later the following morning, so it didn't matter if it took some time to fall asleep.

However, if you enjoy going to work early, it can be beneficial for HSPs to start the day in a peaceful manner with few distractions. By the time the other employees arrive, you have already calmly started your day. You may then be able to go home early, before rush hour traffic, and have an opportunity to take a nap or take a walk in a park after work. You can explore with your boss if you could do some work from home, which is ideal for the HSP. More and more people are working part time to full time from their home office, which really lessens overstimulation for the HSP.

Remember that one of the most important factors in job satisfaction is experiencing positive interpersonal relationships at work. You can positively affect your interpersonal relationships at work when you are relaxed. If you're feeling anxious, the tension amongst your colleagues will grow. However, when you are taking regular mediation breaks and utilizing other relaxation methods to create inner-peace, your coworkers will also become calmer. When you keep your sense of humor and smile frequently, your feelings of joy and happiness at work will increase.

Low Self-Esteem and Job Stress

Some people stay stuck in a job that increases their stress because they deeply believe that is all they deserve. HSPs who were told that they were flawed as children may be unconsciously recreating a dysfunctional family at work. Sometimes HSPs with low self-esteem actually become comfortable in an abusive work situation.

Maria, a single HSP woman in her late fifties, worked for twenty-five years as a manager for a major corporation. She told me that she had a painful and abusive childhood, due to her sensitivity. She said that her job was a living hell due to her rude and inconsiderate boss. Besides suffering from anxiety and depression, she developed coronary problems that her doctor described as probably related to stress at work. However, Maria emphatically refused to consider leaving her job for fear of losing her large pension.

I told Maria that if she continued to work under so much stress, she may not be around to enjoy her pension. Once she entered therapy and finally understood why she had become used to working in an abusive environment, she was able to make changes in her life. Maria eventually quit her job and took a teaching position at a junior college. Although her salary and pension were considerably less, her health improved.

There are literally hundreds of interesting, low-stress jobs available if you want to pursue a change in careers. There are many opportunities in life when we're open to new, creative solutions.

Dealing with Challenging People at Work

Many HSPs have told me how difficult it is for them to deal with noisy people at work. Monica, a single woman in her early thirties who worked for a state agency, reported that noise at work distracted her to the point that she couldn't concentrate on her duties. She worked in a small office with another woman who talked incessantly on the phone, describing her personal problems to friends in a loud, abrasive voice. Monica dreaded going to work in the morning and left her job with a tension headache almost daily. Although Monica was furious, she was afraid that if she asked the coworker to be quiet, the strained relationship would worsen.

We explored many options available to Monica to improve her intolerable work situation. For instance, she could wear a headset or earplugs, change the location of her desk, discuss the problem with her supervisor, or transfer to another department. I reminded her that the coworker may not even be aware that her talking was disturbing Monica. However, the colleague could probably subtly pick up Monica's anger, which could make a resolution more difficult. I suggested that Monica befriend the coworker. (A big part of HSP noise problems is when you immediately see another person as the enemy when you are disturbed by their noise).

I then told Monica that once she develops a good rapport with her colleague, she could tell her (or write her a note) that she has a very sensitive nervous system, which makes normal noise sound amplified. Monica needed to emphasize that it was *her* problem and not blame the coworker. She could then offer several options to the colleague to resolve the difficulty, such as suggesting that the woman talk about personal issues during a certain agreed-upon time. During those intervals Monica would be prepared and could take a break, lunch, or focus on work that could be done wearing a headset.

She could also politely ask if the coworker could speak in a lower voice or use another phone for personal calls. Finally, Monica should apologize in advance for any problems that her sensitivity might cause the coworker and tell her how much she appreciates the colleague's willingness to help her. The truth is that if Monica were a non-HSP the coworker probably wouldn't have to make any changes since many non-HSPs can tolerate or do not even notice annoying sounds. If the colleague is amenable to any of the suggestions, Monica could bring her some flowers with a thank-you note to reinforce her appreciation for the coworker's assistance. Monica finally wrote a note to her coworker and worked out a compromise. From then on, the colleague would make personal phone calls only during her lunch hour.

Creating a New, Stress-free Job

Students frequently tell me that they are dissatisfied with their job and want to explore a new field. I always advise them to be practical when pursuing new vocational goals. If you work in a well-paying job, it may not be beneficial to abruptly quit. First, make a list of your transferable skills and analyze how your skills apply to other vocations. Second, I recommend that you begin volunteering in the area that you would like to work in. Volunteering is an excellent way to obtain experience that could lead to a paid job in the future. Another option is to begin working part-time in a new field to determine if it is feasible for the job to turn into a lucrative full-time position.

Research a New Job

Before venturing into a new line of work, perform a labor market survey. Contact at least ten people who work in the field that you want to go into. Ask about current hiring levels, salary, and qualifications, as well as the physical and emotional demands of the job. Spend some time observing the new work environment. As an HSP, it's important to realistically evaluate whether the job is suitable for a sensitive person. Pay close attention to the stimulation level, job pressure, and work hours. Since HSPs generally process information slowly, take plenty of time to perform the labor market survey. Don't become overwhelmed with too much data or rush to make a quick decision.

It's important to work in a field that matches your temperament as well as your interests. You may want to meet with a vocational counselor who can advise you about various career options. You could take an interest test or other vocational tests to determine your abilities and aptitude for various professions. Elaine Aron's informative chapter called "Thriving at Work" in her book *The Highly Sensitive Person* has many additional tips to help the HSP find suitable employment, as well as an excellent summary of tips for employers of sensitive people in the back of the book (1996). If you are not sure of the work options available, you can also look in the yellow pages of the phone book, peruse

O*NET *Dictionary of Occupational Titles* (Department of Labor 2004) at your local library, or do a search online for job listings.

Every HSP is unique. While a high sensation seeking HSP would enjoy moderate stimulation at work, another HSP would loathe the same job. One of my students works as a security guard in an office building at night. She says that it is a quiet and relaxing work environment. However, another student remarked that she would be afraid to work as a guard since someone may try to break into the building. She also mentioned that she would have a difficult time trying to go to sleep right after work. Many HSPs would have difficulty working in a job where the hours constantly change or working the graveyard shift (11 P.M. to 7 A.M.).

Working for Yourself

Self-employment can be an excellent option for HSPs who don't want to work under the pressure of a boss. According to Elaine Aron, "Self-employment is a logical route for HSPs. You control the hours, the stimulation, the kinds of people you deal with, and there are no hassles with supervisors or coworkers." However, she also points out that you have to be careful about being a perfectionist and driving yourself too hard. You also need to be willing to make difficult decisions. Also, you should be careful not to isolate yourself too much. If you work alone, it's important to meet with colleagues regularly for support. Introverted HSPs could also have some challenges with the marketing aspect of self-employment.

Before beginning self-employment, it's important to complete a thorough investigation as to the feasibility of success for your new vocational goal. It's important to choose a field where you won't need to be working 24/7. Ascertain if there is a need for the product or service that you plan to offer in your proposed geographic area. You could then complete a survey to determine the number of other people or businesses that offer the same product or service. Find out what the competition charges and perform a detailed financial plan of all aspects of the proposed business, including pricing, overhead, marketing, and salaries. Then you need to determine how to promote your product or service and become informed about all necessary taxes and licenses that are needed. Finally, determine the amount of time it will take you to complete all aspects of your job. Since many new businesses fail, I recommend that you meet with a vocational counselor who specializes in helping people in self-employment to analyze whether your venture will be successful.

When I worked as an employee for a private company as a vocational rehabilitation counselor, I billed at the rate of fifty dollars an hour, but I only received eight dollars an hour and the company received forty-two. I remember frantically trying to bill for more hours at the end of each month in order to make my quota to maintain my benefits. When the company laid off most of the counselors due to budget cuts, I decided to start my own vocational rehabilitation firm. In this particular situation, I created a home office resulting in my working half as many hours, yet earning three times what I'd made when I was an employee. While not all self-employment results in such a positive outcome, if you pick the right field you may find yourself working in a more relaxed, lucrative position.

Create Enjoyable and Relaxing Work

- Try to develop a positive attitude toward your job by creating enjoyable social interactions, helping others and being enthusiastic about your work.

- Listen to background music that is calming and maintain proper air circulation and temperature.

- Gaze at pictures of natural settings. Bring flowers and plants to work.

- Have juice or herbal tea, healthy snack foods, and uplifting magazines or articles available for you, your clients, or your employees.

- Have a comfortable chair to sit on. If you are sitting all day at work, periodically perform stretches and take short walks.

- Throughout the day do some slow abdominal breathing exercises and take short meditation breaks.

- If you are calm, your coworkers will be more relaxed, creating interpersonal harmony. Don't forget to smile frequently.

- Explore changes in your job schedule such as beginning work later, working from home, or reducing your hours.

- Create a daily work schedule each morning to plan a pressure-free day.

- Employ the suggestions given in this chapter on how to deal with challenging coworkers.

- If you are working in a very stressful job that can't be modified, examine your beliefs and values as to why you continue to work in a difficult situation.

- Investigate new job possibilities that are well suited for your sensitivity.

8

Nurturing the HSP Soul

$\mathcal{O}$ne of the best attributes of being an HSP is your inherent capacity to have deep spiritual experiences. In chapter 1 we discussed that HSPs are more frequently in a theta brain wave state, whereby you are more open to intuitive feelings and picking up subtle vibrations deeply (Robertson 2003). A sense of spiritual well being can help you meet life challenges and feel more optimistic. One study showed that a spiritual orientation helps terminally ill people avoid spending their last months of life in despair (Rosenfeld 2003). A spiritual focus has shown to be a crucial aspect of how well one copes with death. Expanding our natural attunement with spirit also helps cushion the trauma from major difficulties such as physical disease or the death of a loved one.

The more you develop your sense of spirituality, the easier it will be to cope with daily overstimulation. Some of us may have a resistance to pursuing a spiritual path due to early negative religious experiences. You may want to think of spirituality in terms of unconditional love, beauty in nature, or a Higher Power. You may also be more comfortable relating spiritually to a specific religious figure like Christ, Buddha, Mohammed, or Krishna, or to a prophet like Abraham or Moses. I know one person who is an agnostic but acknowledges that there is a mystery to life when he considers the vastness and the order of the universe. I used to be an agnostic when I was younger and remember my beliefs being challenged by a quote that was carved into the desk in my introduction to psychology class that read: "God is dead"-Nietzsche; "Nietzsche is dead"-God.

Essentially, all religions teach the same thing—to love the divine Higher Power and be compassionate to others as well as to yourself. If you put all the spiritual masters in one room, they would agree on everything, but if you put all the disciples in one room they would agree on nothing. The more that we take comfort in the divine presence within, the better able we will be to cope with life challenges. The stable, unwavering love of God gives us succor during stressful times. Although most people are constantly seeking love and approval from others, even if all the people in the world were to love us, we would not get an infinitesimal amount of the bliss that we can receive from divine Love (Amritaswarupananda 1989).

It's important for the HSP to be practical and discriminating when beginning a new spiritual practice. Proceed slowly so that your nervous system doesn't become overloaded with too much energy. Even positive experiences such as profound spiritual experiences, getting married, or starting a new job can be overstimulating for the HSP. Therefore, even during these uplifting times you need to employ many of the same techniques that you use to cope with stress, such as following a daily routine, progressive relaxation, and taking the necessary herbs or supplements.

My spiritual teacher, Ammachi, attracts huge crowds, so I have to plan ahead to deal with all the stimulation at her gatherings. I try to attend the events when the crowds are not as huge and find quiet places to retreat to during the day where I can sit quietly. Even though the programs frequently continue until very late at night, I usually leave early since I do not function well with little sleep. I give myself plenty of time to unwind at night from the stimulation of being in the presence of so many people. However, once I am prepared, I can tolerate the stimulation of being in the presence of such a popular spiritual teacher with so many adherents and have positive, mystical experiences.

Understanding Brings Inner-Peace

Once you understand the nature of people, you will probably gain more serenity in your life. Almost no one loves another more than their own self, and virtually everyone's motivation is based on self-interest (Amritaswarupananda 1989). One HSP told me that she used to become quite upset when people didn't consider her feelings. If a friend didn't call her, she used to feel hurt. Once she realized the nature of people, she began to accept that some people don't take the initiative to stay in touch. When you let go of the attachment to the idea that people should act in a certain way, you can experience more inner-peace. Therefore, by understanding the nature of the world you will be able to act from your inner essence rather than constantly overreacting to the moods of people and ever-changing situations.

While some people may exude unconditional love, many people will treat you nicely because they want something from you. Notice how polite salespeople are when they want you to buy their product. Would the same person behave in such a kind manner if they knew that you had no intention of purchasing anything? Frequently, the person who said they would love you forever is gone when you don't give them what they want. The nature of a human being's egotistical love is conditional. However, divine love, as exemplified by the true saints such as Christ, Buddha, or Mother Theresa is unconditional.

There is a story about a bird that injured its wing and was trying to get across a river. A fox came by in a boat and told the bird that he would take the injured bird across the river. The bird at first was reluctant to get in the boat with the fox, but the fox convinced the bird that he really had good intentions and didn't want to harm the bird. However, when the bird got into the boat, the fox attacked the bird. Since it is the nature of the fox to hunt birds, the fox simply couldn't resist the temptation. Likewise, when you understand the nature of the human ego, which is based on self-interest, as a sensitive person you won't be so disappointed when you realize that some egotistical people are simply not capable of treating others in a compassionate manner.

Our Temporary Sensitive Nervous System

As sensitive souls, it's easy to get bogged down in the little discomforts of life and forget that what seems so important today will hardly matter next month or next year. Once you deeply understand that your soul's brief journey in this incarnation will pass by swiftly, you won't get caught up in the delusion that you are only this sensitive body. There's a beautiful line in a poem by the Persian poet Rumi that exemplifies the transitory nature of the body, "You are in your body like a plant is solid in the ground" (Barks 1999).

One HSP, Barbara, told me about an epiphany she experienced as a girl. This realization has helped her cope with her sensitivity because she was able to understand the illusory nature of her existence. Barbara told me that one day when she was nine years old she was standing on her steep, ivy-covered front lawn. Barbara suddenly felt that the house in front of her wasn't really her home. She suddenly realized that her parents weren't really her mother and father, but just her caregivers for a few brief years. In her heart, Barbara felt that she was from a different place, which was full of peace and harmony. She suddenly became completely detached from everyone and everything as she felt waves of bliss flowing through her body. After some time, Barbara slowly returned to body consciousness. When the young bewildered girl tried to explain the experience to her mom, she simply dismissed Barbara's profound spiritual transformation as a dizzy spell. However, Barbara always kept the insightful experience in her heart.

Many people believe that what we see in this ephemeral world may appear real, but it's actually a sort of illusion, since nothing real (everlasting) can be destroyed. While our family, home, and bank account will all disappear when we leave our body, the love that we've shared and our spiritual attunement will last eternally. When we die, our souls will not be black or white, Muslim or Jew, male or female, sensitive or insensitive. When we experience the flow of divine energy connecting all beings, our fleeting differences hidden behind the masks of temporary personalities will become less important.

Detachment and Patience

While it's difficult for sensitive people to remain detached during overstimulation, the more you practice patience, the less minor disturbances will irritate you. There's a story about a guru who had a very obnoxious person living in his ashram. One day, after making everyone angry and probably driving the HSPs crazy, the nasty person left the ashram. The guru ran after the ill-mannered disciple and offered to pay him to return to the ashram so that the devotees could learn the spiritual lessons of detachment and patience. Likewise, the more you can just watch the drama of life unfold around you as if you were in a movie theater gazing at the ever-changing shadows of darkness and light, the more your tranquility will increase.

According to the Indian spiritual teacher Ammachi, "We should be like a bird perched on a dry twig. While it sits on the twig, it may peck at fruit in the tree, but at the same time it will always be alert and ready to take flight. It knows that at any moment the dry twig could snap. Likewise, the world and its objects are like a dry twig in as much as they offer us no lasting support. We must be alert and detached, like the bird, even while we are in the world. Then we can soar up to the heights of spiritual bliss. We can leave our bodies at any moment and should always be aware of our true nature" (Amritaswarupananda 1989). Once we recognize that we are the infinite soul rather than a temporary highly sensitive person, we will open our heart and experience more joy.

You will be able to transcend your temporary challenges as you develop spiritually through, meditation, prayer, reading spiritual books, spending time in quiet, natural environments, repeating a mantra, and spending time with other spiritual seekers and teachers. The more you perform selfless service, helping others, the less you will focus on your own problems as you grow spiritually, serving humanity. Finally, you can also increase patience and detachment by following the serenity prayer dedicated to Saint Francis, "God grant me the serenity to accept the things I cannot change, courage to change the things I can and, wisdom to know the difference."

Feeling Gratitude Expands Our Soul

One of the most important spiritual qualities to develop is gratitude. In chapter 5 I recommended that you write down everything that you're grateful for in your life before going to bed. By focusing on the positive areas of your life, you will gently slip off into sleep on a positive note, rather than taking your worries with you throughout the night. This is also an excellent exercise to perform daily to enhance your spiritual growth.

I received the following anonymous, inspiring e-mail recently:

If you woke up this morning with more health than illness, you are more fortunate than the million people on the planet who will not survive this week.

If you can attend a religious meeting without fear of harassment, arrest, torture, or death, you are more blessed than three billion people in the world.

If you have food in the refrigerator, clothes on your back, a roof overhead, and a place to sleep, you are richer than 75 percent of the people in this world.

If you have money in the bank, in your wallet, and spare change in a dish someplace, you are among the top 8 percent of the world's wealthiest people.

If you can hold someone's hand, hug, or even touch someone on the shoulder, you are blessed because you can offer a healing touch.

If you can read this e-mail, you are more blessed than over two billion people in the world who cannot read at all.

What are you are grateful for in life? Write down the things for which you are grateful. Try this practice each morning and notice how your day becomes more enjoyable.

Showing Appreciation

Sometimes HSPs tend to focus on the little irritations caused by other people. The more you concentrate on the positive characteristics of others, the happier you will tend to be. Use your deep compassion to forgive everyone and open your heart through acts of love and kindness. Whenever I complain about someone's behavior, I feel my energy spiraling downward. I have a friend, Adam, who will ask me not to say anything negative about anyone. I find that I feel so much better after spending time with this friend than when I have been making disparaging remarks about others. Do you have a friend or family member who can remind you not to make any pejorative remarks about people?

There is a magnificent, popular story about a teacher who asked the students in her class to write down one positive quality about each of the other students. When she compiled the list and handed it back to the students, all of the classmates were astounded that the other children liked them so much. Many years later when one of the students was killed in Vietnam, the deceased boy's mother showed the teacher a worn piece of paper that was found in his wallet; the list of all the good qualities the boy's classmates had written about him years earlier. As it turned out, most of the other students told their former teacher at the boy's funeral that they, too, had saved the list of precious compliments. This story is a testimony to the power of love and kindness as well as illustrating how everyone wants to feel loved and accepted exactly as they are.

Although as sensitive people you may experience negative emotions such as fear, anger, hatred, and jealousy more strongly than others, you also can feel love more deeply than most non-HSPs. Since love is the strongest emotion, you can easily tap into the infinite power of divine love to heal your relationships. As you forgive others by tuning into the deep power of love within you, peace emerges like a rainbow after a refreshing rain.

The spiritual teacher Peace Pilgrim, who as an elderly woman that walked alone throughout North America for about thirty years promoting inner and outer peace, believed in the inherent goodness of all people. She would frequently exclaim, "Aren't people wonderful?" She told a story about a woman who was jealous of her and continually tried to hurt her when she was a young woman. However, she met every insult with acts of loving kindness, and after expressing so much genuine love, the woman finally softened and became her friend (Peace Pilgrim 1982). Equipped with your infinite capacity to express compassion, you too can overcome hatred with love as you dive deeply to discover the positive characteristics hidden in even the most insensitive person.

The Innocence of a Child

Many spiritual teachers emphasize that we need to have the innocence of a child to grow spiritually. As adults we frequently become
focused solely in our mind as our ego judges everyone and everything.
The ego/mind can block our inherently pure, childlike innocence from
emerging. In our attempt to feed the ego by constantly seeking recogni-
tion, we lose our openness to the divine. Become a zero—then you're a
hero (Amritaswarupananda 1989).

A child is spontaneously open to life. Notice how sweetly and easily
children who don't know each other will begin playing together without
any preconceived egotistical judgments. I want to share a letter that rep-
resents the innocence of children (Zeff 2002). I received it from a boy who
attended a spiritual gathering where I was a counselor several years ago.

Hi Ted,

*School is good, and my favorite subject is math. I have a few
personal questions I am wondering if I could ask you.*

*I am wondering if you can tell me what's it like to die,
because I am kind of afraid.*

*I am also wondering if I'll ever see my Grandma again.
She passed away two years ago, and when I think of her I get
sad because I miss her and would like to see her.*

*When I die, can I be an angel with God up in heaven or
come back as a little boy's guardian angel? Maybe I can be a
guardian angel for a little boy like me who is also scared, so
that I can help him.*

*Is it okay to want something other than God—like
wanting to be a famous football player or like going in a store
and seeing something I like and is it okay to want it?*

Your dear friend,
Daryl

I was touched by the boy's innocence and spontaneity and
attempted to respond to his letter from my heart.

Dear Daryl,

I'm also afraid to die because I don't know exactly what it will be like. However, my dad died two months ago, and I experienced in deep meditation that my dad seemed full of joy after he left his body. I've talked to many people who have had similar experiences, sensing that their loved ones are very happy. So, even though it is scary to die, everything I've experienced and read from the great saints says that the soul will be happy when it leaves the body. It's kind of like having an old car that doesn't run so well anymore, so we have to trade it in for a new model.

I also miss my dad, which is a natural response when someone close to you passes away. While you may not be able to see your Grandma, she may still be able to watch over you and help you from the other side, like a guardian angel. I believe that we will "see" our loved ones again, but maybe in a different form.

Maybe you'll be a guardian angel at some time. The important thing is to be kind and loving to people and then you will be a guardian angel on Earth for many other scared little boys now.

Of course it's fine to want to be a famous football player or want something in a store. However, just remember that everything comes from the divine and to thank God for all his gifts that he's given you. Frequently I've seen famous athletes thanking God for their talent. By the way, God wouldn't have created nice things in the store if He didn't want you to enjoy them. Enjoy everything, live in the present, and don't worry, be happy. God loves you very much as well as your family, friends, and me.

Ted

As an innocent, sensitive child, your vulnerability may have made you believe that there was something wrong with you, especially when people told you the falsehood that you were terrible for being too sensitive. Jay, a highly sensitive man in his forties, told me a story about how a kind sixth grade teacher helped him realize that his sensitivity didn't mean he was a bad person. His family, peers, and other teachers had told him that his introverted and sensitive behavior was disgusting, especially for a boy. Unfortunately, he believed all those lies and came to regard himself as an awful person.

One day his sixth grade teacher asked him to stay after school when she noticed that he was walking around the playground alone and forlorn during recess. He told his teacher that the other boys didn't want to play with him since he preferred gentle games and all the boys only wanted to play football. When he played hopscotch or jacks with the girls, all the other children would tease him, so he walked alone on the playground. His teacher told him that he was very special for being so sensitive and that he would help many people throughout his life since he was so kind. She told him that the other children were wrong for making fun of his gentle nature.

When the teacher told Jay that he was a good person, he disagreed and said it was not true since his parents, brothers, and the other children had told him that he was repulsive for being so sensitive and shy. This compassionate teacher began praising Jay for the remainder of the school year in front of the class, telling him how wonderful he was for being sensitive. As Jay shared this touching story, he became teary-eyed, reminiscing that his teacher was the only person who ever told him that his sensitivity helped him be a worthwhile human being. Like Jay's teacher, you can become a beacon of light for unhappy, sensitive children, praising and appreciating their gentle and sweet nature.

A Metaphysical Perspective

Acupuncture has shown that there are pathways throughout the body that need to be open so that energy isn't blocked. Research has shown that there are seven energy centers in the human body (Myss 1996). HSPs tend to have their higher energy centers open, while the lower ones may be closed. When highly sensitive people live solely from the upper three energy centers of the crown (top of the head), the third eye (the point between the eyebrows), and the throat region, they are constantly absorbing other people's energy. When the lower energy centers in the area of the abdomen, base of the spine, and the area slightly below the base of the spine are closed, the HSP may not be grounded. By opening the lower energy centers, the HSP will become more centered, allowing for a flow of energy throughout the body. This balanced energy flow will help you be better able to cope with stimuli. The centering meditation described in chapter 2 is especially helpful for becoming grounded. You may also want to put heavy (grounding) oils such as sesame oil on your lower energy centers or eat cooked root vegetables, which can help you feel centered.

Some HSPs have reported finding solace in some of the beliefs of Eastern philosophies based in Buddhism or Hinduism. From that perspective, any suffering that people experience in life is due to negative karma acquired during this life or from previous incarnations. All the positive events in life are based on the merits one has gained in this or in previous lives. Looking at your situation from that viewpoint, you might consider that perhaps you were an insensitive person in a previous life and due to the acquired karma, now you must experience a sensitive nervous system in this life. From a Western perspective, many HSPs have also found comfort realizing that they will reap the results of their good actions. We can always lessen the effects of our karma during challenging times by performing good deeds, prayer, and meditation. While sometimes we may despair that our sensitivity is creating many challenges in life, the perceived obstacles can be opportunities for us to grow closer to God.

Meditation, Nature, and Your Spirituality

Many spiritual teachers have taught that the purpose of being born human is for our individual soul to expand into God's infinite love and light. Through meditation and spending time in nature, highly sensitive people can easily experience the divine effulgent energy flowing through us. Throughout this book we have discussed the benefits of meditation. Through inner contemplation and reflection, we can develop our innate spiritual ability and calm our nervous system. I have observed many of my HSP students experience a phenomenal spiritual transformation after leading them in a guided meditation. They may come to class feeling agitated, but after even a short meditation, the HSP easily enters into a calm and blissful state.

Although your sensitivity to noise and frequent thoughts, may distract you during meditation, you can still receive many benefits by integrating this practice into your daily life. You never know when you will be blessed with a profound spiritual experience. Sometimes I have suddenly experienced feelings of bliss even during a restless meditation.

When you practice meditation on a regular basis, you will be able to experience your soul's connection to the divine and your mundane sensitivity challenges will pale in comparison. Even if you don't have profound spiritual experiences, meditating lets your consciousness momentarily transcend this temporary Earth plane as you dive deeply into spirit.

Spending time in nature can also awaken your innate, spiritual qualities. Your highly sensitive nervous system will easily relax when you spend time in the calmness of nature. In an urban environment, it is easy to become deluded, believing that it's natural to sit in traffic jams on freeways, inhale toxic pollution, and listen to cars honking. In a bucolic countryside, you can feel your connection to the divine more deeply.

Since as an HSP you have the capacity to feel more joy and appreciate beauty deeply, you can instantaneously enter into a tranquil state when you spend time in a lovely natural environment. Your soul spontaneously soars upward toward a divine state as you observe the harmony in nature. Also, you may be subtly inspired realizing the unselfish quality of nature. For example, an apple tree gives all its fruits to others, taking nothing for itself even when it's being chopped down (Amritaswarupananda 1989).

There Is No Death

The thought of death can sometimes be frightening for some HSPs. Since many of us have spent a lifetime trying to control an abundance of irritating stimuli, we may fear what will happen to us when we leave our sensitive bodies. Will we be disturbed by overstimulation on the other side? The good news is that since there will be no "time" on the other side, we won't have to worry about time pressure, and I don't think that there are any annoying cell phones in heaven. Seriously, I doubt that our sensitivity challenges continue when we leave the body.

The fear of death can also be caused by the thought that death is going to destroy everything that you have—all that you are attached to and all that you cling to. That clinging causes pain. If you can let go of all your attachments, then dying will not be scary (Amritaswarupananda 1989). From a reincarnation perspective, getting old and approaching death is a win-win situation for a spiritual aspirant since you will either be closer to obtaining a new, healthy body in a new birth or will merge for eternity in God's love.

Most people spend lots of time and money trying to look attractive by dieting, buying stylish clothes, paying beauticians to dye their hair, and joining expensive health clubs. However, I feel that our consciousness will make a quantum spiritual leap when we realize the absurdity of how we try to increase our ego by beautifying our bodies, which will end up buried or just a pile of ash in a few short years (Zeff 2002). Sometimes we don't listen to our inner-guidance and believe the non-HSP values as we sacrifice our emotional and physical health in order to earn money, status, and fame. There is a bumper sticker that reads, "the one who dies with the most toys wins." However, the person with the most toys at the end is still dead and may take the karma they have created with them into their next level of existence.

When we identify with only our physical form, we're vulnerable to fear about its destruction. However, when we feel that our inner-essence will remain, we're less afraid. In a mere one hundred years, all of us who have been desperately trying to protect our sensitive bodies will have passed away from the Earth. However, when we meditate on the thought that our true essence will continue to exist, a deep sense of inner-peace can arise.

When we were discussing the fear of death in one of my classes, Alan told me how he almost drowned as he was swimming in the Pacific Ocean. A powerful rip tide pulled him out to sea, and Alan said that he was losing his strength to stay afloat as he gasped for air. As huge waves continuously knocked him under the water, he thought that his death was imminent. The class was surprised to hear that in the middle of his ordeal Alan began laughing as he recognized that the problems that had seemed so important to him earlier in the day now had no significance.

Alan was saved at the last minute, and watched as his illusory worries slowly crept back into his consciousness as the day progressed.

While we may intellectually understand and believe that the soul continues after death, we naturally become emotionally distraught when friends and relatives die. One HSP told me that her nervous system was literally thrown into a state of shock when she received the news of her mother's death. HSPs often grieve harder, so expect to sob deeper than your non-HSP friends. During these traumatic times, you really need to utilize all the calming techniques that have been discussed in this book.

I'd like to share with you how I, as a highly sensitive man, used my compassion, sensitivity, and innate spiritual strength to deal with my father's passing a few years ago. When I heard that my dad was dying, I immediately went to the nursing home and filled his room with lovely flowers, my dad's favorite classical music concertos, and read poems from his beloved books of poetry. I tucked my dad into bed with a lovely purple, blue, and magenta afghan my grandmother knitted for her young son almost a century earlier. Even though I was sorrowful, I took solace in the blessed way my dad was leaving his body. He rested in a sunny room filled with bouquets emanating sweet scents while listening to magnificent sonatas and surrounded by friends and family telling him how much they loved him.

My dad's condition remained stable for a few days, but he still slept most of the time. Even though he was in a deep sleep, I felt that on a subtle level his soul could still hear me reading the uplifting poetry, which he had cherished throughout his life. I began reading a poem by Edna St. Vincent Millay entitled *My Candle Burns At Both Ends,* "My candle burns at both ends, it will not last the night,". . . suddenly, I heard my dad's voice weakly, whispering the rest of the poem by heart, "it will not last the night, but ah my foes, and oh, my friends, it gives a lovely light" (Sullivan 1978). While I contemplated that he may not last the night, I was grateful that he had given off such a lovely light throughout his life.

The little glow of the body may be extinguished, but I prayed that his soul would merge with the eternal light of the divine. When I returned home exhausted that night, I immediately fell into a deep sleep, only to awaken a few hours later with an excruciating pain in my left leg. During the last few weeks of his life, my dad complained of the severe pain that his nearly gangrenous open wounds on his left leg caused him. The sharp pain in my leg was almost unbearable, but it only lasted for a few moments. As soon as the pain dissipated, I felt myself floating in space, being drawn toward a deep, luminescent blue and silver light. It was the most indescribably beautiful vision that I had ever beheld. Simultaneously, a deep feeling of freedom and joy enveloped my entire being. After some time in this blissful state, I realized that my dad must have just left his body. I fell back asleep, and when my nephew called me in the early morning to tell me that my dad passed away at 12:30 A.M., I realized that was the exact time that I had experienced my astral journey.

When you are born into this world you do not bring anything with you. When you leave the earth, only the merit of selfless actions and love that you have shared will accompany you on your final journey (Amritaswarupananda 1989). As you grow spiritually and maintain an awareness of the temporary nature of the world, your sensitivity becomes a joy and you will be able to spread love and compassion to all sentient beings and help uplift suffering humanity. As long as you focus on the luminous divine energy flowing through you, practice the coping techniques in this book and love, and approve of your sensitivity, you will experience joy and tranquility for the rest of your life and throughout eternity.

$$9$$

Answering Common
Questions from HSPs

$\mathcal{T}$his chapter includes questions from HSPs, followed by direct answers. I chose questions that can help you implement many of the suggestions that I've made throughout this book. Even if some of the questions aren't specific to your situation, this chapter will help you learn by example how to make positive changes. The format of this section will be different from the rest of the book since it contains only questions and answers. It is still a good idea to jot down the answers that you would like to integrate into your life.

Question: *I have lived alone in my comfortable New York apartment for twenty-three years. Last year some highly insensitive people moved in above me. They play loud music till all hours of the night. I can still feel the bass reverberating in my ears. Besides blasting the music, they stomp around all night long which sounds like a herd of elephants. When I asked my rude neighbors to turn the music down and to walk more softly, the man swore at me and* *slammed the door in my face. I am petrified that this man may attack me. The apartment manager said that the rude neighbors blamed me, saying the music wasn't loud and no other neighbors have complained. I'm afraid to call the police since he threatened that if I bother him again I would be sorry. I'm having trouble functioning on my job due to lack of sleep. Those vile neighbors keep me up all night! My health is beginning to suffer, and I feel like I'm having a nervous breakdown. Don't suggest that I move since I am in a rent-controlled apartment and can't afford to pay current rents. I won't consider moving from New York either. What can I do?*

Answer: As an HSP, I can really empathize with your situation. Apartment living for sensitive people can be very challenging. You can either try to befriend the insensitive neighbor, ask the apartment manager or police to intervene, or make changes within your living situation. If all attempts to remedy the situation fail, you have to ask yourself if it is worth it to have your physical and mental health deteriorate just to remain in your home. There are always options—you are never stuck.

I recommend that you see a professional counselor to help you deal with this untenable situation. If you don't have the funds to pay for a private therapist, there are low-cost clinics available in every community. You may want to investigate if it's really true that you can only live in New York, that there are no other apartments you can afford, and that you really need to live alone. You may want to investigate why you're holding onto these beliefs and how you would feel if you gave them up. Although I have always hated to give up the security of my own safe space, I've come to learn that there is always another comfortable home waiting for me when I'm open to the possibility of change.

Question: *My roommate is driving me crazy. She comes in late every night when I'm asleep and begins banging around in the kitchen. My room is next to the kitchen, and I've told her that she wakes me up when she cooks late at night. She says that she is trying to be quiet, but that my sensitivity is restricting her lifestyle. I also can't stand the odors that come into my room from the kitchen after she cooks and the bright light seeping into my bedroom under the door.*

Answer: I'm not sure how you got into such a difficult living situation, but it clearly isn't working for you. As an HSP, you must be vigilant in interviewing potential roommates and thoroughly investigate any future house for potential noise, odors, and light problems. HSPs really need to have a quiet, dark, and odor-free room. You could try to work out a compromise such as having your roommate cook earlier and you doing the dishes the next morning or possibly changing rooms with her. You could look into insulating your room to minimize noise, light, and odors. If a compromise doesn't work, you will have to consider changing roommates or moving. It's a good idea to make a list of everything you need in order to feel comfortable at home. Then carefully make sure each of your criteria is met before moving into a new home.

Question: *My neighbor always parks his ugly pickup truck on the street in front of my house creating an eyesore for me whenever I sit on my living room couch. I've asked him nicely several times to please park the vehicle just ten feet away, but he refuses. He told me that I don't own the street. What can I do?*

Answer: If you have already asked your neighbor nicely and he has refused, you may want to investigate why he doesn't want to park his car away from your living room window. Maybe he feels that you're imposing on him or is angry with you for something else. He just may be a rude, insensitive person. However, you can try befriending him by helping him as a neighbor.

If he refuses to move the vehicle, you will have to surrender to the situation since, ultimately, we can't change anyone but ourselves. When someone infringes on your space, it could trigger a lot of anger, perhaps reminding you of your childhood when you were helpless and your space was violated. Examining the original source of the frustration can help you resolve the inner-conflict. On a practical level, you may want to plant a beautiful large flowering bush by the window that would obstruct the eyesore or move your couch so you're facing a picture of a lovely nature scene. You could purchase two sets of curtains for your window and keep the lower one closed to avoid looking at the monstrosity, yet let light into the room with the upper curtains open. I wouldn't recommend escalating the conflict by trying to block the space or calling the police. The last thing an HSP needs is to worry about an angry neighbor attacking them.

Question: *I have a neighbor who was very noisy and we got into quite a battle over loud music that he refused to turn down. After the manager made him* *turn down his music, he ended up moving to another apartment in the same building, but whenever I see him he always gives me dirty looks, which really irritates me. What can I do to make him stop?*

Answer: Although your neighbor may have been 99 percent at fault in the disagreement, if you were a non-HSP you may not have been bothered by his loud music. You were likely angry when you told him to turn down the music or when you reported him to the manager. He may have felt attacked by you. He was the one who had to leave his home due to your demands. I recommend that you use the 1 percent apology technique with him, either verbally or in a written note. Apologize for your 1 percent responsibility in the dispute. Tell him that if you didn't have a sensitivity to noise, there wouldn't have been a dispute and apologize for any inconvenience that you caused him. The chances are high that if you apologize, he will eventually stop giving you dirty looks and both of you will feel more at peace.

Question: *You keep emphasizing the need to slow down and create a peaceful environment at work as a way to reduce stimulation for the HSP. However, I live in the real world where I need to make enough money to support my wife and two children. I have to commute an hour to work and am always under a lot of pressure at work to meet quotas. I come home late every night feeling exhausted and tense. Your plan sounds nice if you can afford the luxury of not working, but that is not an option for me.*

Answer: It sounds like you believe that you have no choice in life; that you must push yourself to work in a pressure cooker. You may want to examine where you acquired the belief that you have to work under such austere and tense circumstances. What were the values that your parents, friends, and teachers instilled in you that helped create your belief system? Is it really true that the job you have is your only option to support your family?

I had a student who worked under similar circumstances, and he would tell me during each class that he couldn't leave his job. He worked as a chef in a fancy restaurant, and his high salary helped pay for his high monthly rent in San Francisco. He worked for many hours, six days a week, under constant pressure. His intense work schedule contributed to his severe insomnia, ulcers, and migraines. Each week in class he emphasized that he could not afford to quit his job since he was supporting his wife and two young children.

In each weekly class, as he examined whether it was really true that he had to continue in the stressful job, he came to realize that the physical and emotional deterioration the job created in his life was simply not worth it. Once he changed his consciousness and realized that he deserved a happy life, he found a lower paying yet stress-free job in a rural location where the housing costs were a fraction of what he had been paying. Later I heard from this student that within months of quitting his job, his insomnia, ulcers, and migraines virtually disappeared. When we are aware of our mortality and the temporary nature of the body, we begin to understand the true goal of life, which is developing inner-peace.

Question: *Part of my job is answering the phone on the first ring, so I can't implement your suggestion of using the phone as a cue to relax, letting it ring three or four times. I don't have the time to take a few, slow, deep breaths, repeat a mantra, and visualize my muscles relaxing. I like the idea of remembering to relax at work when the phone rings, but I don't think it's feasible in my current job.*

Answer: The ringing of the phone can still be a cue to take at least one slow, deep breath and relax your muscles while you simultaneously reach for the phone. Try to schedule short meditation breaks throughout the day and a longer one during your lunch hour. Even meditating and practicing progressive relaxation for a few minutes hourly will have a significant beneficial effect on your psychological and physiological health. If your employer won't let you take a short break every hour, perhaps you should look for a more HSP-friendly position.

Question: *I work in a very stressful office in Chicago, and a coworker at the desk next to mine is extremely noisy. I tried explaining to her that I am an HSP and she ridiculed me, asking what doctor diagnosed me. She said that I was too demanding and shouldn't let things bother me. She yells at me in her abrasive voice to get over it whenever I ask her to speak more quietly, stop chewing gum loudly, or turn down her radio. Now I never want to tell anyone that I'm an HSP.*

Answer: There are approximately fifty million HSPs in the United States and hundreds of millions of us throughout the world, so while we are a minority, we are a very large minority. Out of approximately 250 million non-HSPs in America, you dealt with one very insensitive person. My experience has been that the vast majority of non-HSPs were empathetic when I have explained that I have a sensitive nervous system. If you had one bad experience with a rude doctor you would probably not say that you were never going to see a doctor again. Don't let one person deter you from speaking your truth. You may want to even show your coworker Elaine Aron's book *The Highly Sensitive Person* (1996). However, it's important to use discrimination as to whom you tell about your trait. You could try befriending and working out a compromise with your coworker, wearing a headset or earplugs, changing your desk, discussing the problem with your supervisor, or finding another job.

Question: *I have to travel a lot for my job, making at least two or three business trips a month. I have a hard time when traveling on planes with crying babies, people kicking the back of my seat, or sitting near passengers with strong perfumes.*

Answer: It can be challenging for HSPs to travel by plane due to the overstimulation and proximity to so many people. You're going to have to be prepared before making a trip and assert yourself on the plane. As soon as you notice that you're sitting next to someone with a strong perfume, tell the flight attendant that you have a chemical sensitivity and need to change seats. As soon as someone is kicking the back of your chair, politely ask the person to stop. If you cannot change your seat when sitting near crying babies and loud passengers, you can listen to soothing music on a headset or the plane audio system. You may also want to put on earplugs or a sleep mask. You can take breaks by standing near the bathroom or walking down the aisle. When you can't change your outer circumstances, you can always surrender to the situation, realizing that the challenges will be over in only a matter of a few hours.

Question: *My husband likes to go out on weekends while I need to relax at home. He's very action oriented and always likes to try the latest craze, from rock climbing to hang gliding. I have no desire to participate in any of those weird activities on weekends. He criticizes me, telling me I'm selfish not to come along with him on his latest stunts. We end up constantly arguing, and I'm afraid our marriage is doomed. There is no way I'm going to go along with* *his frenetic need to always be stimulated, and there is no way he will stay home with me.*

Answer: I recommend that you read *The Highly Sensitive Person in Love* by Elaine Aron (2001). The author enumerates many methods to help the HSP/non-HSP couple create a positive relationship. I noticed that you called his interests "weird" and you implied there is something wrong with him for his high sensation seeking desires. It sounds like both of you may be negatively judging each other and not accepting your unique differences.

The key to creating a loving relationship is compromise and acceptance. Both people at times need to push themselves to engage in activities that they wouldn't normally do. Although you mentioned that you like to relax at home, perhaps you can also enjoy going for a relaxing walk in a park or having a picnic after he finishes a stimulating activity such as rock climbing. Likewise, your husband could perhaps engage in some stimulating activities at home. Perhaps you could design some furniture that he could build. If you both compromise and come from a place of love and acceptance, the relationship can thrive.

Question: *I want to do calming activities in the evening to reduce the stress of my day, but as a mother of a two year old I find it impossible to implement any of your suggestions. I can never fully relax since I never know when my baby will start crying or need my attention. My little boy tends to get upset easily and the least little thing seems to set him off. I love my son dearly, but at the same time I really need down time, which is simply not possible now.*

Answer: From the description of your son, he may be highly sensitive too. I recommend that you read Elaine Aron's book *The Highly Sensitive Child* (2002). The book is full of excellent suggestions on raising a highly sensitive child from birth to maturity. It's important for you to get a lot of support from family, neighbors, and friends. How much time is the father helping out? Do you have parents or other family members who can support you? Have you tried to look for other mothers of two year olds for support?

While it's true that being "on call" twenty-four hours a day with a toddler can make it difficult to implement many of my stress-reducing techniques, during certain times of the day you can still have a little free time to practice relaxation techniques. Throughout the day you can always perform slow, abdominal breathing whenever you're feeling over-stimulated. Keep the awareness that with each passing year you will need to be less "on call" with your son. Try to really enjoy the positive aspects of your son's age and appreciate the all-too-fleeting toddler stage. Time marches on very quickly, and before you know it your son will be attending school. In only fourteen years, he'll be asking you for the car keys!

Question: *I never felt like I fit in with my family, who are all non-HSPs. Every year when I visit my relatives during the Christmas holidays, the trip becomes tortuous, since I have no time to be alone. I have to share a room with my sister and there is literally nowhere for me to escape to get peace and quiet. My parent's small house is filled with people constantly chattering away. I dread going to my parent's house for Christmas, yet I don't want to be alone during the holidays.*

Answer: Next year, before you visit your family, it's important for you to let them know what your needs are. If your relatives cannot provide you with a safe, quiet space, it would be better to either stay in a nearby motel or invite your family to visit you, whereby you can decide the parameters of the interaction. While it's true that you can't dictate how your parents should run their household, you have a right to request what you need for your sensitivity. If your relatives won't accommodate your special needs as an HSP or if you can't stay in a nearby motel, you have to ask yourself if it's worth the emotional strain to stay in such an inhospitable environment. Perhaps you can create a new, more enjoyable Christmas celebration with friends.

Question: *I become extremely agitated when I closely follow the news. I even have nightmares about terrorist attacks. However, I can't seem to stop keeping up with world events even though it seems to make me feel anxious. Throughout the day I find myself either reading the newspaper, watching the news on TV, listening to talk radio, or surfing the Internet for the latest breaking news.*

Answer: I have twelve words that will help you: Turn off the media; turn off the media; turn off the media! No matter how much you want to change, negative environmental influences will permeate and influence your consciousness. Unfortunately, when you are out of balance, you crave the things that will make you more out of balance. Just as an alcoholic has difficulty abstaining from drinking if they spend time in a bar, you cannot be calm when you immerse yourself in the negative news media. Your media addiction could be as emotionally destructive to you as alcohol is for the alcoholic. You could benefit from the support of individual or group counseling.

I'm not suggesting that HSPs shouldn't be informed about world events. Spending five or ten minutes each day checking the headlines is fine as long as it doesn't negatively affect you. However, when following negative news reports creates anxiety or depression, it's time to turn them off. Remember to ask yourself when you're watching the murderer of the day on television, would you invite him into your home if he knocked on the door? Absolutely not! So please don't invite assassins into your home via the media.

Question: *My neighbor's daughter was murdered a few years ago walking down a street at night in a major city. Her death has really affected me. I'm more afraid to go outside, and I find myself in an almost paranoid state, seeing everyone as a potential murderer. The reality is, bad things do happen to good people in this dangerous world, and as a sensitive person, I'm really frightened.*

Answer: Yes, bad things sometimes happen to good people. However, most serious assaults on strangers take place in or near dangerous neighborhoods very late at night. Also, most murders are committed by people they already know (family members, acquaintances). As an HSP, the chances are infinitesimally small that you would attract such violent people into your life. If you use discretion and take practical precautions such as driving with your doors locked and avoiding dangerous neighborhoods at night, you need not hide in your house fearing imminent danger. You probably have a greater chance of accidentally injuring yourself at home than being assaulted while shopping during the day at the mall. Sometimes people also tend to attract what they fear. So it's important to focus your consciousness on attracting loving and harmonious people into your life.

Question: *I have terrible difficulties falling asleep. I am trying to follow your suggestions for reducing insomnia by going to bed earlier and not looking at the clock. You say it's best not to look at the clock after 8 P.M. and to go to bed by*

10 P.M. How do I know what time it is if I'm not supposed to look at the clock, and how do I set my alarm clock?

Answer: You can set your alarm clock before 8 P.M. and estimate when it's approximately a couple of hours after 8 P.M. to go to bed. However, don't create negative self-talk by thinking that it must be 11 P.M. or even midnight so you have to hurry up and fall asleep. After 8 P.M. your focus should be on just relaxing by meditating, reading an uplifting book, taking a warm bath or by doing progressive relaxation exercises with a tape or by yourself. Time is a major negative hook that creates sleep challenges. No time, no problem. As you become relaxed in the early evening, your body and mind will naturally become drowsy as you slip off into a deep, peaceful sleep.

Question: *I'm going to a private school where I'm studying to be a graphic artist. As an HSP I tend to process things slowly. My teacher constantly tells me that I'm working too slowly. He has scolded and humiliated me in front of the class, announcing that I'm an awful student for taking so long to complete my assignments. He is quite immature and bullies his students with sarcastic remarks when we make mistakes. The director of the school has told me that I'm talented in graphic arts and has been supportive of my work. However, I'm afraid that if I speak up to either her or my teacher, he will make my life a living hell. I need to take several more classes with this highly insensitive teacher in order to graduate.*

Answer: Since your teacher appears to be an insensitive bully, telling him that you are an HSP may not help. Since you seem to have the support of the director of the school, you may want to discuss the situation with her. You can explain that you are afraid that if the director chastises the offending teacher, he will make your life more miserable. Perhaps you can suggest to the director that he create general guidelines for how teachers should treat students so the offending teacher won't feel that it's personal. You may want to show the director the "List of Tips for Teachers" from *The Highly Sensitive Person* (234). Since approximately 15 to 20 percent of the population is highly sensitive, there are probably other HSPs in the class whom you can talk to for support. I'm sure other students are offended by his rude behavior. Your teacher seems like a very unhappy person, and you may even want to practice feeling compassion for this pathetically out-of-balance person. By cultivating compassion for your teacher, you will elevate your consciousness to a higher state and won't be dragged down to his level of behavior.

Question: *I become extremely anxious whenever I have to go for a blood test. Many years ago I fainted, and I'm afraid that I'll pass out when I get a blood test. Just the thought of someone sticking a needle into my arm and taking out blood can make me break out in a cold sweat. I have always overreacted to needles, even as a child. What makes this worse is that I am a male, and men are supposed to be tough, so I become extremely embarrassed and ashamed of my weakness. I avoid going for blood tests and to doctors, even though I know I need a physical exam. What can help me?*

Answer: First of all, you're not alone in feeling anxious or faint when going for a blood test or an injection. Many HSPs, men and women, have a difficult time with doctor visits and laboratory procedures. The hospital and medical environment is quite emotionally challenging for the HSP.

When you have to go for a blood test tell the phlebotomist that you tend to become faint and need to lie down or rest in a reclining chair. You can explain to the lab technician that you are an HSP and would greatly appreciate their compassion and understanding. Also, never watch when the lab technician is drawing blood or when you receive an injection. It can also help to engage the phlebotomist in a conversation to take your mind off the procedure. By the time you've finished talking, the lab procedure will have been completed.

Before leaving for the lab or doctor's office you can take an herbal formula or allopathic medication to reduce your anxiety. If you are taking a fasting blood test, bring a piece of fruit to eat after the test to increase your energy and blood-sugar level. Finally, do not rush out of the lab, which can create anxiety. Rest for a few minutes with your eyes closed, meditating or planning your day. When you feel centered, slowly get up and leave the lab.

By the way, real men and real women sometimes faint. There's nothing wrong with you, just with people who perpetuate false judgements that men aren't supposed to faint. Just think, there probably would be an end to war if there were more men who fainted at the sight of blood!

Question: *I stopped going to the movies because I can't stand it when people sitting near me talk or eat loudly. The noise drives me crazy and I can't focus on the movie. My wife likes going to the movies and gets upset when I tell her I'd rather wait for the video to come out and watch the flick in the peace and sanctity of my own home.*

Answer: In a theater full of hundreds of people you are bound to have some people who are not considerate of other patrons. You may want to avoid crowded theaters so that you can easily change your seat if your neighbor is noisy. Theaters are less crowded if you wait until a new movie has been out for several weeks or if you go to the movies on weekdays before 6 P.M. Attending a movie premiere on a weekend night is an invitation to HSP hell.

If you can't find a quiet seat, you can always report excessive noise to the manager. I remember having to speak to a manager about some parents who allowed their baby to cry throughout the movie. That solved the problem.

I have an HSP friend who once told me that he got so upset with so many people in the audience talking at a movie, he screamed in a loud voice, "Would everyone just be quiet." He then told me that the entire audience fell silent. However, if you plan ahead, you won't have to yell at the audience to quiet down.

Question: *Noisy people at restaurants really upset me. I pay good money for a nice meal and then frequently have to listen to a stranger's personal discussion, which ruins the dining experience for me. I can't stand it when people speak in a loud, abrasive voice. Nowadays, even when customers are dining alone, they are often shouting into their cell phone. In addition, many restaurants have music that is so loud you can hardly hear your dining partner. Also, I hate dining out during the summer when I'm likely to have a freezing air conditioner blowing on me.*

Answer: Some restaurant reviewers now rate the noise level of restaurants. Choose a restaurant that you know is generally quiet and try to sit at a table away from noisy people. When you are deeply engaged in a discussion with your dining partner, you won't notice the conversations of other customers as much. Try to eat out before or after the peak lunch or dinner crowd. Also, you can always ask the manager to change your seat or turn down the music or the air conditioning. It may be less disturbing for you to get the food to go and savor the delicious repast in the sanctity and solitude of your own dining room.

Many years ago I wrote a restaurant guide and dined at over three hundred restaurants. I noticed that the managers really listened to feedback from their customers and tried to please their patrons, so don't hesitate to ask the manager to help create a pleasant dining experience.

Question: *You mentioned that as an HSP we should wear earplugs or a headset in noisy, public places, such as in waiting areas of an airport. However, I don't like to feel disconnected from people. When I really want to withdraw from our overstimulating world, I'll go on a retreat. However, being around many people talking loudly really gets on my nerves.*

Answer: Maybe you can actually tune into people more by wearing earplugs or a headset in noisy environments. When you're feeling angry with noisy people, you may be actually tuning them out. But as you find yourself insulated from their noise, you may even feel free to smile at the people who are talking loudly. One HSP student, Claire, told me that when she was at a restaurant recently, she was annoyed by a woman sitting alone at another table who was talking in a loud, abrasive voice on her cell phone. Claire became so angry that she almost asked this woman to be quiet. But instead of focusing on the boisterous customer she put on her headset and listened to some pleasant music. As the noisy woman was leaving the restaurant, the woman smiled at Claire and Claire was able to smile back. Instead of creating a possible contentious interaction, by efficiently masking the din, Claire was able to have a positive interaction.

Question: *I would like to try meditation, but I've heard that some people have had bad reactions to it, and I'm afraid that I may not be able to emotionally handle it. What if I go crazy if I try to meditate?*

Answer: While a very small percentage of people may have had a negative reaction to meditation, I've never witnessed this in any of my hundreds of students. Before you begin a meditation practice, you may want to discuss it with your doctor. You can begin meditating by simply breathing slowly and relaxing your muscles for a few minutes with your eyes closed. If you have a positive experience, slowly increase the time that you meditate. You can also listen to a guided meditation or relaxation tape. It would be very unusual for you to have an adverse reaction from performing slow abdominal breathing and relaxing your muscles.

In fact, I think that people can go crazy if they *don't* meditate. In the last century alone, humans killed a hundred million other people in wars. As long as the ego/mind identifies with fulfilling endless outer desires, anxiety, tension, and destructive behavior increases. When you meditate and experience your true inner-nature, which is beyond the temporary ego, a sense of deep peace emerges.

Question: *It seems that you emphasize the need to meditate to feel serene, yet it's difficult for me to sit still with my eyes closed. My body becomes very antsy, and I have to move around. My mind is constantly jumping all over the place. I feel hopeless that I can't implement this important technique to calm myself down. What should I do?*

Answer: First of all, if it's difficult for you to meditate, don't feel guilty about it. You may want to do some form of gentle exercise prior to meditating, such as yoga or going for a walk. Hatha yoga was created to calm the body and mind to help you easily enter into a deep state of meditation. You may want to take a hatha yoga class and then try meditating at the end of the class.

If you are still experiencing difficulties relaxing in meditation, you can listen to a meditation tape so that you are being guided into a quiet space. It may be easier for you to just spend a few moments every hour taking a few slow deep breaths as you let your muscles relax deeper and deeper with each exhalation. You can also try a walking meditation, repeating, "I am calm" or "I am peaceful" with each footfall. You may want to alternate your sitting and walking meditation. Even if your mind is jumping like a monkey from branch to branch, you're still receiving many physical, emotional, and spiritual benefits by even briefly disengaging from the overstimulating world.

10

Choosing the Right Healer for You

There are so many healing techniques advertised today that you can easily become overwhelmed trying to choose the appropriate modality to help you cope with your finely tuned nervous system. Do you remember the cartoon I described in chapter one about the woman who became so overwhelmed trying to choose from a multitude of toothpaste brands that she had to go home to lie down? Likewise, you may find yourself inundated with a plethora of healers, therapies, books, supplements, and herbs that claim they will help.

Choose Carefully

Each HSP is unique. A method that helps one HSP could have an adverse effect on another. I recommend that you consult with a holistic medical doctor before starting any alternative healing program (information about how to find a holistic doctor can be found later in this chapter). You need to carefully review each modality and use your intuition to decide which therapy is best for you. It would be good to spend some time reflecting on each of the descriptions listed below and note if any of the methods seem to resonate with you. There are many types of healing therapies, so I have not been able to list all of them. If you are interested in a therapy that has not been presented, please use the same criteria to investigate whether it is appropriate for you.

Of course, the quality of treatments and practitioners necessarily varies, so I can't promise that the one you choose will meet your expectations. As with any treatment, allopathic or alternative, it is up to you to select carefully and with as much knowledge as possible. I believe the information in this chapter will be a good start to your research.

Acupuncture

In this ancient Chinese system of healing, thin needles are inserted into particular points of the body, which can increase the immune response and alleviate pain by balancing the flow of energy throughout the body (Weil 1995).

Some HSPs may have an adverse reaction to acupuncture due to the slight pricking sensation when needles are inserted. It's important for highly sensitive people to interview an acupuncturist before their first treatment to determine if the practitioner is gentle. Some acupuncturists insert needles in the body so deeply that the patient may experience a sharp pain, while other practitioners are so gentle that the patient feels virtually no sensation. You may also want to consider acupressure or shiatsu, both of which use pressure from the practitioner's fingers and hands to stimulate points on the body, relieving pain and stress. It's important to let the therapist know if the pressure is too strong.

For assistance in finding a qualified acupuncturist contact the American Association of Acupuncture and Oriental Medicine at 888-500-7999 or www.aaom.org.

Aromatherapy

This branch of herbal medicine uses the inhalation of essential oils extracted from plants and herbs for healing purposes. The inhalation of fragrances like lavender, jasmine, or rose can help create a peaceful atmosphere on an emotional level. The absorption of chemicals of the essential oils into the blood stream, lungs, and sinuses can help heal some physical illnesses.

Although aromatherapy is an excellent approach to calm down the HSPs nervous system, individuals who are sensitive to fragrances may have a deleterious reaction to the treatment. Before you buy an aromatherapy pot and essential oils you may want to test the procedure, as well as the essential oils. Often, displays of "tester" sample bottles are available where aromatherapy essential oils are sold. The tester display can be a valuable source of information. You may also want to consult with an aromatherapy practitioner. To find one, contact the National Association for Holistic Aromatherapy at 888-275-6242 or www.naha.org.

Ayurveda

Ayurveda is a five thousand year old system of healing from India. During an ayruvedic consultation, a practitioner evaluates each individual's constitution and creates a specific treatment plan based on the patient's constitution. Then the practitioner makes specific recommendations to restore harmony in the patient, which could include diet, herbs, exercise, yoga, herbal steam baths, oil massage, and lifestyle changes.

Many of the suggestions in this book are based on the ayurvedic principles of living a harmonious lifestyle in an out-of-balance world. Most HSPs have a vata constitution, which tends to be more sensitive to stimuli. I highly recommend this holistic healing system for HSPs. To find an ayurvedic healer, contact:

Ayurvedic Institute at 505-291-9698 or www.ayurveda.com

Ganesha Institute at 800-924-6815 or www.healingmission.com

Maharishi Ayurveda at 800-255-8332 or www.mapi.com

The Chopra Center at 760-931-7566 or www.chopra.com

Biofeedback

Biofeedback is a technique where a practitioner hooks you up to monitors that gauge your basic physiological responses, such as your heart rate or skin temperature. During the session, you can check the readings on a monitor to learn how to control your response to stimuli. Once you learn how to regulate your body's vital functions, you can reduce stress and pain.

While biofeedback training is generally enjoyable and relaxing, some HSPs may feel uncomfortable being hooked up to machines with wires. You may want to visit a biofeedback clinic and become familiar with the procedure before starting your own treatment. While you may feel a little uncomfortable while being hooked up to a machine, once you begin the treatment you'll probably be able to enter into a very relaxed state.

Find a qualified biofeedback practitioner by contacting the Biofeedback Certification Institute at 303-420-2902 or www.bcia.org.

Bodywork

Muscle tension can lead to chronic patterns of stress and pain by compressing nerve fibers. Therapeutic massage relaxes muscles, relieves pain, and has a sedative effect on the nervous system (Goldberg 1993). It's crucial for an HSP to tell the massage therapist what degree of pressure is comfortable. And remember, due to your openness you can easily absorb the energy of the massage therapist, so interview the therapist before agreeing to receive a massage and make sure you're okay with their attitude and energy. Since some HSPs don't feel comfortable being touched by strangers, they might opt to receive massages from a partner or a close friend. There are too many different types of bodywork to describe them all here, but I've included a partial list.

Some Examples of Body Work

Feldenkrais is a system of movements, floor exercises, and bodywork designed to retrain the central nervous system. This method is used to help find new pathways around any areas of blockage or damage to the body and helps people move more easily by learning smooth and fluid movements. This therapy seems to be very well suited to the HSP because of its gentle, natural, and soothing effect. HSPs can tap into their intuition to help facilitate an awareness of subtle changes in habits and movements during the process.

Trager is a very gentle form of bodywork that uses gentle rocking and bouncing motions to induce deep relaxation. The therapist gently loosens tense muscles and stiff joints. Trager is also used to help facilitate the nervous system's communication with the muscles, which can help people with chronic neuromuscular problems. This is a gentle approach that is suitable to most HSPs.

Rolfing is an invasive form of bodywork that aims at restructuring the musculoskeletal system by manipulating patterns of tension deep in the tissues. Rolfing can release repressed emotions as well as dissipate habitual muscle tension. It may seem strange that I listed an invasive form of bodywork here, but I thought it was important to let you know that there are some forms of massage that may go too deep to help those of us with a sensitive nervous system. Although I wouldn't recommend this treatment for most HSPs, if you can tolerate deep bodywork, it could be quite helpful for releasing emotional and muscle tension.

To find a qualified body worker, contact:

American Massage Therapy Association at 847-864-0123 or www.amtamassage.org

Feldenkrais Guild at 503-926-0981 or www. feldenkrais.com

International Rolf Institute at 303-449-5903 or www.rolf.org

Trager Institute at 415-388-2688 or www.trager.com

Chiropractic

Chiropractic doctors make adjustments of the spine and joints that can influence the nervous system. These adjustments can promote healing for the back as well as other physical problems. However, many HSPs may find the adjustments too jarring and invasive for their sensitive nervous system.

Nevertheless, there are gentle forms of chiropractic adjustments available. Network Spinal Analysis is a form of neurological work that brings about a deeper level of healing, getting past physical, emotional, and mental traumas to help you develop new strategies to handle the stresses of daily life more effectively.

Directional Non-Force Technique (DNFT) incorporates gentle, precise adjustments to muscles, tendons, vertebrae, and discs using the body's wisdom as a guide and can be effective in restoring joint function as well as returning the body to optimal well being. Most HSPs could benefit from both of these gentle forms of chiropractic adjustment. Find a practitioner by contacting:

> American Chiropractic Association at 703-276-8800 or www.acatoday.com

> Association for Network Chiropractic Spinal Analysis at 303-678-8086 or www.innateintelligence.com

> Directional Non-Force Technique at 310-657-2338 or www.nonforce.com

Counseling

Counseling or psychotherapy can help the HSP cope with the challenges of living in an over-stimulating non-HSP world. You may want to see a licensed psychologist, a licensed marriage and family counselor, or licensed social worker. If you can't afford to pay for private therapy sessions, virtually all cities have low cost therapy clinics (check your phone book for your city or county department of mental health). You may also want to participate in a supportive group therapy program.

How do psychotherapy and counseling differ? You might think of them as a continuum. At the counseling end, you will receive information, advice, and tips for carrying out what you have learned in this book. However, you need to work from the psychotherapy end of the continuum if you are feeling recurring inappropriate emotions (depression, anxiety, anger) that are interfering with your life, or you have not been able to apply counseling suggestions.

When choosing a counselor or therapist it's important to interview several carefully to determine which one feels right for you (for example, behavioral, Jungian, etc.) and if the person is empathetic toward HSPs. You wouldn't buy the first car that you looked at. You will be trusting your mental health to the professional that you choose and living with all the effects of your choice for at least as long as you would own a car. So don't just answer their questions, but formulate some good questions of your own and listen carefully for both knowledge and support of your sensitivity.

Although group therapy can be a beneficial process, some HSPs may feel overwhelmed, shy, or uncomfortable in a group setting. A group should have a sufficient number of HSPs, and the facilitator needs to be very supportive and skilled in working with HSPs in a group setting. There may be groups for HSPs in your area, or you may want to follow Elaine Aron's model in *The Highly Sensitive Person's Workbook* for starting your own HSP discussion group (1999).

Get help in finding a therapist or an HSP group in your area by contacting:

American Psychological Association at 800-374-2721 or www.apa.org

HSP classes at www.hspsurvival.com

HSP annual gatherings at www.lifeworkshelp.com

Internet HSP discussion groups at www.sensitiveperson.com

Flower Remedies

Flower remedies utilize the essence of flowers to help psychological and physical healing. The flower remedies are taken in a tincture (liquid)

form. One of the most well known formulas, Rescue Remedy, has a calming effect in emergency situations. Taking tinctures of flower essence is generally safe, but as with herbs, the sensitive person should take low dosages in the beginning. Some HSPs have reported that Rescue Remedy is so helpful in stressful situations that they regularly carry it with them.

Learn more about flower remedies by contacting the Flower Essence Society at 1-800-736-9222 or www.flowersociety.org.

Herbal Medicine

Although herbs are generally safe for reducing stress and treating disease, I recommend that you consult with a holistic medical doctor who has botanical training before taking herbs. A consultation will help you avoid any possible adverse reactions. You may also want to meet with a practitioner of ayurveda, Chinese medicine, herbology, or naturopathy. It's important that the practitioner is knowledgeable about any harmful reactions from herbs or combining herbs with allopathic medicine. Please refer to chapter 4 for more information on herbs for the HSP.

To help find an herbalist, contact The American Herbalists Guild at 770-751-6021 or www.americanherbalistsguild.com.

Holistic/Alternative Physicians

Holistic/alternative physicians are medical doctors who have received training in either herbal or Chinese medicine, supplements (such as vitamins, minerals and amino acids), nutrition, homeopathy, or acupuncture. The advantages in consulting with a medical doctor is their knowledge of the side effects of taking herbs and supplements and their ability to order appropriate diagnostic tests. Get more information about finding a holistic/alternative doctor by contacting:

American Holistic Health Association at 714-779-6152 or www.ahha.org

American Holistic Medical Association at 505-292-7788 or www.holisticmedicine.org

American College of Advancement in Medicine at 800-532-3688 or www.acam.org

International Society for Orthomolecular Medicine at www.orthomed.org

Homeopathy

Homeopathic medicine utilizes highly diluted remedies made from natural substances that catalyze natural healing responses in the patient. Many homeopathic remedies can promote calmness and tranquility. Homeopathy has been used extensively in England for many years.

To avoid any adverse reactions, you may want to consult with a medical doctor with homeopathic training or make sure that the practitioner is knowledgable about any potential side effects. Most homeopathic practitioners object to their patients using many other forms of treatment, including allopathic drugs and herbal formulas since they may cancel out the remedy. Although homeopathy is generally safe, the HSP still needs to use caution when utilizing this method.

To find out more about homeopathy and finding a practitioner, contact the National Center for Homeopathy at 703-548-7790 or www.homeopathic.org.

Hypnotherapy

Hypnotherapy encourages patients to enter a state of heightened suggestibility, at which point suggestions can be introduced. These suggestions can help you change your behavior or beliefs and help you relax. Hypnotherapy can be effective in treating stress, anxiety, fear, and depression and help the client increase a tolerance to negative stimuli.

Although the client has to be willing to participate in the process for hypnosis to work, some HSPs may experience fear of being out of control during hypnosis. I recommend that the HSP meet with the hypnotherapy practitioner several times to become familiar with the process. It may be too overwhelming for some HSPs to be hypnotized without carefully understanding and becoming familiar with hypnosis. However, once HSPs become comfortable with the procedure, anxiety due to overstimulation can be reduced.

For help finding a qualified hypnotherapist, contact the American Society of Clinical Hypnosis at 630-980-4740 or www.asch.net.

Meditation

During meditation one is not reacting to the past or worrying about the future. Concentrative meditation focuses the attention on the breath or a mantra (words). Mindfulness meditation involves being a witness to the mind without reacting (Goldberg 1993).

There are many schools of meditation that teach both concentrative and mindfulness meditation. Investigate any meditation technique thoroughly before committing to beginning a regular practice. You need to use your discrimination and intuition to select the approach that is most in tune with your sensitivity.

There are too many methods of meditation to list here but a few popular and effective concentrative forms are: *Integrated Amrita Meditation Technique*, which is a very effective method to experience deep relaxation, especially if you have difficulty concentrating. *Transcendental meditation* (TM) is a simple mental technique that is usually practiced for twenty minutes twice daily. Many scientific studies have shown that during TM, the body gains a deeper state of relaxation than during ordinary rest (Goldberg 1993). *Self-Realization Fellowship* also teaches several valuable meditation techniques that help create inner-peace and joy.

One popular form of mindfulness meditation is Buddhist meditation, which focuses on paying conscious attention to one's breath and posture as well as thoughts that arise in the mind. Thich Nhat Hanh offers beneficial retreats in mindfulness meditation that deeply calms the nervous system and helps the meditator live in the present moment. Finally, *Vipassana meditation* is another valuable form of mindfulness meditation that helps create deep inner-peace.

For more information, contact:

Integrated Amrita Meditation Technique at 510-537-9417 or www.amma.org

Transcendental Meditation at 888-532-7686 or www.tm.org

Self-Realization Fellowship at 323-225-2471 or www.yoga nanda-srf.org

Buddhist meditation at 978-355-2798 or www.buddhanet.net

Mindfulness Meditation at 802-436-1103 or www.plumvil age.org

Vipassana Meditation at www.inquiringmind.com

Naturopathy

Naturopathic practitioners aid the healing process by incorporating a variety of alternative methods including diet, herbs, and lifestyle changes based on the client's needs. Naturopaths treat the cause rather than the effect of being out of balance (Goldberg 1993). This gentle, holistic healing modality could be helpful for most HSPs. For information contact the American Association of Naturapathic Physicians at 1-866-538-2267 or www.naturopathic.org.

Physical Isolation Tank/ Flotation Tank

The physical isolation tank is a structure that is made out of cardboard or wood and a plastic liner, measuring seven feet by four feet and is four feet high. It is totally dark inside the tank, and when a person's ears are immersed in the ten inches of saline solution, it is also soundproof. The tank cuts out all stimuli from the senses as one floats supine with the entire body on the surface of the saline solution in the womb-like environment.

The stimuli-free atmosphere could be beneficial for HSPs. How-ever, some HSPs may become frightened floating in salt water in the dark or may find the salt water irritating. It's important to enter the flo-tation tank after thoroughly investigating and understanding how the tank works. During the first session you may want to spend just a short time in the tank to acclimatize yourself to the new environment and learn how you can open the door to leave whenever you want. Once you begin to feel secure in the stimuli-free environment, you will experience very deep levels of tranquility.

For more information, look up www.floatation.com/wheredetails.html#USA.

Further Reading

This section contains a list of books that you may find helpful to imple-ment your coping strategies as a highly sensitive person.

Ayurveda: The Science of Self-Healing (1984) by Vasant Lad describes the healing system of Ayurveda, which can help the HSP live a harmonious life.

The Highly Sensitive Person (1996) by Elaine Aron is the seminal book about HSPs, and is another must read for any highly sensitive person.

The Highly Sensitive Child (2002) by Elaine Aron is a must read for any-one raising or working with highly sensitive children.

The Highly Sensitive Person in Love (2001) by Elaine Aron succinctly describes the highly sensitive person in intimate relationships, with many suggestions for interacting with HSPs and non-HSPs.

The Highly Sensitive Person's Workbook (1999) by Elaine Aron offers spe-cific exercises for reframing your life as an HSP, many suggestions for coping, and information on how to start your own HSP discussion group.

You Can Heal Your Life (1987) by Louise Hay is a valuable book for healing emotional and physical problems, with helpful information on changing habits by using affirmations.

Loving What Is (2002) by Byron Katie offers a self-inquiry process to cope with difficult situations by accepting reality.

Making Work Work for Highly Sensitive People (2004) by Barrie Jaegger offers HSPs strategies to build confidence, combat stress, and find work that is emotionally, financially, and creatively rewarding.

The Power of Now (1999) by Eckhart Tolle helps the reader find inner-peace by focusing on the present moment.

Peace Is Every Step (1991) by Thich Nhat Hanh is one of many books by the Buddhist teacher with many insightful techniques for creating tranquility through mindfulness and being focused in the present.

Perfect Health (1991) by Deepak Chopra is an excellent book by the internationally known medical doctor on how to lead a healthy and harmonious lifestyle based on Ayurveda.

Searching For God, Part I (1997) by Ted Zeff is the inspiring story of an HSP's spiritual journey.

Searching For God, Part II (2002) by Ted Zeff is the continuation of the inspiring story of an HSP's spiritual journey.

Spontaneous Healing (1995) by Andrew Weil is one of several books by the well-known doctor of alternative healing, offering natural healing techniques that can be very beneficial for the HSP.

Stop Aging Now (1995) by Jean Carper shows the effectiveness of supplements, herbs, and foods that can help HSPs with weak immune systems or suffering from stress-related diseases.

HSP Web Sites

www.hsperson.com Elaine Aron's Web site contains information about books on HSPs, the newsletter "Comfort Zone," and updates about annual gatherings.

www.hspsurvival.com Ted Zeff's Web site with information for HSPs on coping strategies, a healing program for HSPs on CD, and individual instruction.

www.hspwork.com Barrie Jaeger's Web site offers HSPs strategies to find work that is emotionally, financially, and creatively rewarding.

www.lifeworkshelp.com Jacquelyn Strickland's Web site includes information about living as an HSP and an annual HSP gathering.

www.highlysensitivepeople.com Jim and Amy Hallowes' Web site, which offers advice on how an HSP and non-HSP couple can deal with the challenges they face.

www.sensitiveperson.com Thomas Eldridge's Web site includes HSP businesses and professional directory, a book and links page, and a message board.

Conclusion

While this book is now coming to an end, your journey toward inner-peace is just beginning. I am confidant that as you slowly begin to integrate some of the suggestions in this book, you will experience more joy and tranquility in your life. Remember that you are not alone. There are millions of highly sensitive people in every country who are also trying to cope with a sensitive nervous system. Now that you have the coping skills to survive in our overstimulating world, you can truly enjoy being a highly sensitive person.

My best wishes are with you for a life filled with good health, inner-peace and joy.

References

Amritaswarupananda, Swami. 1989. *Awaken Children: Dialogues with Ammachi, Volume I*. Kerala, India: M.A. Mission Trust.

———. 1994. *Ammachi: A Biography*. San Ramon, CA: M.A. Center.

Aron, Elaine. 1996. *The Highly Sensitive Person*. New York: Carol Publishing.

———. 1999. *The Highly Sensitive Person's Workbook*. NewYork: Broadway Books.

———. 2001. *The Highly Sensitive Person in Love*. New York: Broadway Books.

———. 2002. *The Highly Sensitive Child*. New York: Broadway Books.

Barks, Coleman and John Moyne. 1999. *Open Secret*. Aptos, CA: Threshold.

Becker, Marty. 2002. *The Healing Power of Pets*. New York: Hyperion.

Bhat, Naras. 1995. *How to Reverse and Prevent Heart Disease and Cancer*. Burlingame, CA: Kumar Pati.

Carper, Jean. 1995. *Stop Aging Now*. New York: Harper Collins.

Chopra, Deepak. 2001. *Grow Younger, Live Longer*. New York: Three Rivers Press.

————. 1991. *Perfect Health*. New York: Three Rivers.

————. 1994. *Restful Sleep*. New York: Three Rivers Press.

Cook, Kathy. 2001. Ryan's well. *Canadian Reader's Digest* January 2001.

Cousins, Norman. 1983. *The Healing Heart*. New York: Norton.

Dalai Lama and Howard Cutler. 2003. *The Art of Happiness*. New York: Riverhead Books.

DeGrandpre, Richard. 1999. *Ritalin Nation*. New York: W W Norton.

Federal Drug Administration. 2003. Report on mercury measurements in 39 seafood varieties.

Field, Tiffany. 2000. *Touch Therapy*. New York: Harcourt Brace.

Frawley, David. 1989. *Ayurvedic Healing*. Salt Lake City, UT: Morson.

Friedman, Meyer and Ray Rosenman. 1974. *Type A Behavior and Your Heart*. NewYork: Fawcett Columbine.

Glass, D. C. and M. L. Snyder. 1974. Time urgency and the Type A behavior pattern. *Journal of Applied Psychology* 4:125.

Goldberg, Burton. 1993. *Alternative Medicine: The Definitive Guide*. Tiburon, CA: Future Medicine.

Hanh, Thich Nhat. 1991. *Peace Is Every Step*. New York: Bantam.

Hay, Louise. 1987. *You Can Heal Your Life*. Santa Monica, CA: Hay House.

Jacobs, Gregg. 1998. *Say Goodnight to Insomnia*. New York: Henry Holt.

Jaeger, Barrie. 2004. *Making Work Work for Highly Sensitive People*. New York: McGraw-Hill.

Katie, Byron. 2002. *Loving What Is*. New York: Harmony Books.

Kindlon, Dan and Michael Thompson. 1999. *Raising Cain*. New York: Ballantine.

Kivel, Paul. 1992. *Men's Work*. Center City, MN: Hayeldon.

Lad, Vasant. 1984. *Ayurveda: The Science of Self-Healing*. Wilmot, WI: Lotus Light.

Murray, Elizabeth. 1997. *Cultivating Sacred Space*. Novato, CA: Pomegranate Press.

Myss, Caroline. 1996. *Anatomy of the Spirit*. New York: Three Rivers Press.

Peace Pilgrim Friends. 1982. *Peace Pilgrim: Her Life and Work in Her Own Words*. Santa Fe, NM: Ocean Tree Books

Pelletier, Kenneth. 1977. *Mind as Healer, Mind as Slayer*. New York: Delacorte.

Pollack, William. 1998. *Real Boys*. New York: Random House.

Ramakrishna Swami. 2003. *Racing Along the Razor's Edge*. San Ramon, CA: M.A. Center.

Rosch, Paul. 2003. Report on stress. *American Institute of Stress*. Yonkers, NY.

Rosenfeld, Barry. Having a sense of spiritual well-being. *The Lancet Journal* May, 2003

Roskies, Ethel. Effectiveness of an intervention program for coronary-prone managers. *Journal of Behavioral Medicine* June, 1979.

Sullivan, Nancy. 1978. *Treasury of American Poetry*. Garden City, NY: Doubleday

Tolle, Eckhart. 1999. *The Power of Now*. Novato, CA: New World Library.

U.S. Department of Labor. 2004. *O*NET Dictionary of Occupational Titles*. Indianapolis, IN: Jist Works.

Wallace, Keith. 1970. The effectiveness of the transcendental meditation program. *Science Magazine* 167:1751–1754.

Weil, Andrew. 1990. *Natural Health Natural Medicine*. Boston: Houghton-Miffler.

———. 1995. *Spontaneous Healing*. New York: Knopf.

Whitaker, Julian. 2001. *Reversing Diabetes*. New York: Warner Books.

———. 2004. Serious problems reported with supplements. *Medical Alerts* 14:7.

Worwood, V. 1997. *The Fragrant Mind*. London: Bantam Books.

Zeff, Ted. 1981. *The Psychological and Physiological Effects of Meditation and the Physical Isolation Tank on the Type A Behavior Pattern.* Ann Arbor, MI: University Microfilms.

———. 1997. *Searching For God.* San Ramon, CA: Shiva Publishing.

———. 1999. *Healing Insomnia Home Study Guide.* San Ramon, CA: Zeff Publishing.

———. 2002. *Searching For God, Part II.* San Ramon, CA: Shiva Publishing.

Some Other
New Harbinger Titles

Surviving Your Borderline Parent, Item 3287 $14.95

When Anger Hurts, second edition, Item 3449 $16.95

Calming Your Anxious Mind, Item 3384 $12.95

Ending the Depression Cycle, Item 3333 $17.95

Your Surviving Spirit, Item 3570 $18.95

Coping with Anxiety, Item 3201 $10.95

The Agoraphobia Workbook, Item 3236 $19.95

Loving the Self-Absorbed, Item 3546 $14.95

Transforming Anger, Item 352X $10.95

Don't Let Your Emotions Run Your Life, Item 3090 $17.95

Why Can't I Ever Be Good Enough, Item 3147 $13.95

Your Depression Map, Item 3007 $19.95

Successful Problem Solving, Item 3023 $17.95

Working with the Self-Absorbed, Item 2922 $14.95

The Procrastination Workbook, Item 2957 $17.95

Coping with Uncertainty, Item 2965 $11.95

The BDD Workbook, Item 2930 $18.95

You, Your Relationship, and Your ADD, Item 299X $17.95

The Stop Walking on Eggshells Workbook, Item 2760 $18.95

Conquer Your Critical Inner Voice, Item 2876 $15.95

The PTSD Workbook, Item 2825 $17.95

Hypnotize Yourself Out of Pain Now!, Item 2809 $14.95

The Depression Workbook, 2nd edition, Item 268X $19.95

Beating the Senior Blues, Item 2728 $17.95

Call **toll free, 1-800-748-6273,** or log on to our online bookstore at **www.newharbinger.com** to order. Have your Visa or Mastercard number ready. Or send a check for the titles you want to New Harbinger Publications, Inc., 5674 Shattuck Ave., Oakland, CA 94609. Include $4.50 for the first book and 75¢ for each additional book, to cover shipping and handling. (California residents please include appropriate sales tax.) Allow two to five weeks for delivery.

Prices subject to change without notice.